BHAGAWAD GEETA THE GATEWAY TO FREEDOM

PRABHA DUNEJA

Presented by :

GEETA SOCIETY
2822, Camino Segura,
Pleasanton, CA 94566, U.S.A.

ISBN : 81-7077-081-5
First Edition : April, 2002
Second Edition : Jan., 2005

Translation and Roman Transliteration
of the Sanskrit Text with
Comprehensive Introduction

by :
PRABHA DUNEJA
Tel. : 925-484-5411; Fax : 925-417-5946
e-mail : duneja@aol.com
Web. : www.holygeeta.com

Publisher :
GOVINDRAM HASANAND
4408, Nai Sarak, Delhi-110 006 (INDIA)
Tel. : 91-11-23977216
e-mail : ajayarya@vsnl.com
Web : www.vedicbooks.com

Printed at :
RADHA PRESS
2465, Main Road, Kailash Nagar, Delhi-110031 (India)

YOURS TO YOU

ACKNOWLEDGEMENTS

I want to express in few words my heart felt gratitude to the holy sages of the past and present and the other several *Geeta* scholars, whose teachings have inspired me to present this translation from the Sanskrit text with comprehensive introduction of *Bhagawad Geeta*— The song of the Supreme Divinity.

I feel immensely indebted to my husband Amritji and our son Anshuman for their genuine encouragement and sincere support in the completion of this noble work. I am especially grateful to my respected grandparents Sri & Smt. Ganga Ramji and my parents Dr. & Mrs. Manohar Lalji and my uncle Prof. Nand Lalji, who initiated me into the study of *Bhagawad Geeta* at the early age of eight. I want to thank sincerely to Mrs. Manorama Iyer, who worked very patiently in typing the preliminary work. Special thanks to Swami Jagdishwaranand Saraswatiji who edited the translation and also provided some valuable suggessions.

—*Prabha Duneja*

PUBLISHER'S NOTE

The Publisher feels honoured in presenting ***Bhagawad Geeta - The Gateway to Freedom*** in complete English translation with detailed introductory essay, by Mrs. Prabha Duneja, an educationist and devotee of Lord Kṛṣṇa.

Prabha has authored a number of books. Her clarity of vision about the teachings of the *Geeta* and her humility make her a great teacher. She comes from a family of Vedic scholars, specially her father and uncle, who dedicated their whole lives to the study and preaching of the *Veda* and *Vedanta.*

She is blessed with special gifts and talents and is a featured speaker at temples, churches, schools and at conferences, introducing the Vedic Philosophy and the message of the *Geeta* in U.S.A. and other parts of the world.

I am sure that this elegant handy edition will receive the same warm reception from the general public, as the author's earlier works.

—Publisher

FOREWORD

The modern age is, no doubt, a scientific age. Science has provided the modern man all to make his life comfortable, but still there is a cruel paradox of material plenty without an iota of mental peace. How can a harmonisation be brought about in this clash of the objective opulence and subjective poverty, *Geeta,* the dialogue between Śrī Kṛṣṇa and Arjuna, in the battle-field of 'Mahābhārata' war, provides the answer.

In this small booklet, Mrs. Prabha Duneja, with her erudite scholarship, and above all, with the kind grace of God Almighty, has explained the essential message of Bhagawad Geeta in such a remarkable manner that the laymen as well as learned, anywhere on this earth, would find her work most enlightening as well as inspiring.

With blessings,

—M. Gopal Swami Saraswati

CONTENTS

INTRODUCTION

Bhagawad Geeta, the song of the Supreme Divinity is the holy dialogue between Arjuna and Lord Kṛṣṇa. It is the personal communion of the human soul with the Supreme Soul. It is the communication of *Nara* with his eternal companion *Narayana;* where the human soul brings forward a question O'Lord please enlighten me about my *Dharma* and how can I live in peace and harmony with my own inner-self, with others and with nature. *Geeta* presents the picture of a deep psychological conflict between the conditioned ego-centric self and the Higher-Self which is ultimately resolved with an alignment with the source of life. It gives profound insight into the working of human psychology and makes it very clear that every person creates his own limitations, problems, whims and fantasies. Most of these whims are the dictates of his mind and ego. His bondage is the product of the functioning of 'I'-ness. In general the interpretation of the whole situation is based on how he selects and processes his incoming thoughts. When he resorts to the Supremacy of the Higher-Self he goes beyond his limitations and comes to the realization that he is much more than his mind, body and ego. He experiences for himself that the notions of his assumed limitations exist only in the dimensions of his psychological and physical self. The moment he transcends his limited boundaries of false identifications a miraculous transformation takes place instantly which leads him gradually but effectively out of bondage to a new plateau where there is freedom from all anxieties and fears. The old emotional conflicts become less important and slowly seem to fade away in the mist of past. This is indeed the systematic conceptualization of the inherent potentials and introduction to the mysteries of the Higher-Self. This psychological approach of Sri Kṛṣṇa has touched the hearts of millions and has aroused a genuine love, devotion and respect for Him. Throughout the dialogue, the love and care of *Narayana* (God) for *Nara* (human soul) becomes more explicit and personal. This psychological intimacy and mutual closeness of the spirit with the human being is what makes the dialogue specially interesting.

Throughout the dialogue Arjuna is guided step by step through the conditioned intrigues of mind into the clear and precise understanding of the Self which opens the doorway to Self-realization, God-realization and liberation. The entire approach towards various facets of Arjuna's problems is very natural, psychological, practical and profound. Right in the first chapter when Arjuna expresses his deep sorrow on the painful memories of past and his concern about his relatives Sri Kṛṣṇa, the knower of human psychology, remains silent. He listens peacefully the long lecture of escapism from Arjuna. He doesn't show any sign of appreciation, sympathy or criticism. Sri Kṛṣṇa knows when a person is depressed and speaks in confusion and self-pity he should be allowed to speak, and until he is ready to listen no comments should be made. Sri Kṛṣṇa also knows that a deluded and confused person who is disintegrated, makes lofty statements according to his point of view which are generally self-contradictory and irrelevant to the situation at hand. Arjuna's arguments are hollow, extremely sentimental and highly emotional. He continues to speak in utter depression and Sri Kṛṣṇa listens calmly until Arjuna requests for guidance and becomes receptive to suggestions. This systematic and simple approach of Sri Kṛṣṇa in counselling Arjuna to the realization of his inborn duty makes the study of the Holy sermon very rewarding. Sri Kṛṣṇa knows very well that Arjuna's refusal to engage in war is futile and meaningless because his inborn nature *(swabhāva)* will compel him to fight. He emphasizes the fact that the strongest desire of every human being is to express himself genuinely. It is the manifestation of his inborn disposition that gives him maximum satisfaction and fulfilment in life. He reminds Arjuna about his love for archery and how he has always aspired to become the greatest warrior of the world. How much he has enjoyed being a soldier and to dedicate his life for the welfare of his kingdom, justice and righteousness. Sri Kṛṣṇa tells Arjuna that turning away from his assigned duty as a soldier will haunt him for the rest of his life and he will always live in guilt and shame.

Although in the beginning the conversation is grounded in tension because of Arjuna's poor response but gradually and slowly Arjuna becomes receptive to the teachings. His faith is strengthened and Sri Kṛṣṇa's Divinity is revealed to him. Arjuna comes to the realization that he is actually a co-sharer in accomplishing the restoration of *Dharma* and orderliness in times of great chaos in society.

The dialogue includes in depth the psychological effects of teachings on human consciousness and the subjective changes that occur with devoted and receptive attitude of Arjuna. Throughout the long conversation between Sri Kṛṣṇa and Arjuna, there are other substantive ideas related not so much to the immediate problem of Arjuna but which have a profound bearing on the process of Self-unfoldment and Self-realization. In the words of Dr. Paul Brunton, "Geeta summarizes various approaches to the Overself and also describes the latter. Sri Kṛṣṇa not only represents the embodied spiritual teacher, but He is ultimately the Overself within man, the God within who can illuminate all dark corners and answer all questions. At the end of the dialogue after hearing all the teachings, the pupil's mind becomes peaceful. He says indeed: "My doubts are dispelled. Destroyed are my illusions". By what magic was this mental change accomplished? Through the guidance and grace received from his teacher and his own inner ascent in striving for insight. The difficulties one encounters in modern life can be met and overcome after we gain such insight. Wisdom means the ability to negotiate all the circumstances of life adequately, correctly and with spiritual success. The deep spiritual comfort emanating from the teachings of the *Geeta* is peculiarly needed at this stage of the world's affairs". This psychological approach in *Bhagawad Geeta* has attracted the particular attention of the great educationists of the world. Many psychological concepts determined by the modern psychologists seem quite in conformity with the teachings of the holy dialogue.

Sri Kṛṣṇa enlightens Arjuna about the games

of mind and alerts him about the conditioned experiences of the senses. He tells that when a person screens reality through the ideas which are conditioned with some fixed notion he becomes fragmented and confused. When he goes beyond the intrigues of mind and receives direct guidance from the Higher-Self he is gradually liberated from the deep psychological conditioning. The inner guidance disperses his confusion about the conflicted emotions and he becomes more and more receptive to the call of the Supreme-self. It is indeed so true that without the proper understanding of the self it is not possible for anyone to function properly in any field of life. A person moves in utter confusion in search of something not quite clear to him and the performance of his work explains dissatisfaction, restlessness and inner-emptiness. The radical cure for all these problems is the conscious re-orientation with the indwelling Supreme-Self with faith, willingness and trust. The person has to ask for guidance and make himself receptive to the instruction of the Supreme-Self. Success, creativity, Psychological satisfaction, inner contentment and peace in life are possible only when the inherent potentials are explored systematically.

The knowledge of the Self which enlightens the individual about the real concept of *Dharma* and guides him about the proper functioning in life is experiential. It is not revealed to a person at random, it comes in a very systematic order. It emerges from the deepest awareness and moves through the various levels of consciousness. When the mind turns inward for guidance, the inner chambers of the subconscious mind start opening one by one and the change takes place in the personality step by step. It is the journey from the subtle to the gross, from the subconscious to the conscious and from the unmanifest to the manifested Divinity. Sri Kṛṣṇa counsels Arjuna to rise above the conflicting emotions of both pleasure and pain, gain and loss, victory and defeat, and perform the duty in a balanced state of mind with honest guidance from the Higher-Self. He enlightens Arjuna about the knowledge of the Supreme-self along with the proper understanding of the individual-self. It is through the art of developing a communion with the Higher-Self, the embodied-self becomes enlightened about the various levels of consciousness such as physical-self, psychological-self and the spiritual-self. It is the intimacy with the Supreme-soul which marks the fundamental basis for the acquaintance with everything that exists within and without.

The general theme of the dialogue is the realization of the Supreme-soul through the performance of work in day to day life. The entire message is rooted in devoted performance of action with proper insight and enthusiasm. Sri Kṛṣṇa declares that by being devoted to one's own duty a man attains the highest perfection and spiritual competence. The Supreme Lord of the world should be worshipped through the dedicated performance of one's own duty. It is the attitude of sincere devotion to one's duty that reveals the presence of the Supreme through the execution of work. When a person conducts his personal duty in the spirit of *yajña* (sacrifice) he becomes blessed with the grace of the Divine. To worship Lord through the performance of daily duties is to transform the whole life into the dedicated service of the Divine. Any one who makes himself a conscious instrument in carrying out the work of the Lord in society he can transmute his work into a means for the highest spiritual perfection and freedom. The place of his work becomes the temple of Lord and the manner of carrying his work becomes sacred mode of service. Worship of the Lord through the dedicated performance of one's assigned duty purifies the individual. The pure devoted sincere duty-oriented attitude accelerates his day to day emotions to the realization of the Higher-Self. He lives like a *yogi* in the midst of worldly affairs. *Karmayoga* is a means for the realization of the Divine. It is through *Karmayoga* one can grasp the mystery of the eternal. It brings satisfaction, enjoyment, inner fulfilment and entertainment at the same time. A *Karmayogi* performs his work in a spirit of disciplined dedication, enthusiasm and devotion. His dedicated attitude transforms every bit of work into the *Yoga* of action and prepares him for meditative unity in transcendence. A dedicated *Karmayogi* grows into the most cherished status of saintliness even without his being aware of it.

The message of the holy dialogue has been held in deep interest and reverence by the people all over the world, because it is not addressed to a monk in isolation. The great declarations about the mystery of life, death and rebirth, God and His manifestations which has been discussed in Upaniṣads between the great seers and their disciples in the quietude of the *Āśramas* and monasteries has been brought to the comprehension of an ordinary person living in society. Teachings of *Geeta* present a unique art of living, which can be pursued by each and every person under all kinds of circumstances in life. It gives guidance for living a dynamic balanced life, which is spiritual, peaceful, creative, prosperous and harmonious in all respects. This is indeed the great message of "the Song of the Divine", which is of immediate interest to a married man, a soldier, a doctor, a teacher and a householder. With reference to this, I like the statement made by Dr. Franklin Edgerton in his commentary on *Bhagawad Geeta, "Geeta* provides a religious justification for continuing an approximately normal human life. Therein lies its strength. It does not ask the impossible; and yet it furnishes religious inspiration. It holds out the hope of salvation on terms which are not out of the reach of the great mass of mankind. And it provides for its scheme of salvation a philosophic background, based on commonly accepted Hindu postulates". Sri Kṛṣṇa makes it very clear to Arjuna that unity in *yoga* is not merely a practice in isolation; it is the discipline of living in the awareness of the Supreme Divinity. It is the manifestation of the inner anchorage with Divine in every day life; which can be practiced in almost every station of life, in office, at home, with family, while walking and while performing the most serious duties. That is why Sri Kṛṣṇa repeats again and again the words *"Tasmat sarveshu kaleshu yoga yukto bhava Arjuna"*. O'Arjuna, learn to live in the awareness of the Self, while being engaged in the activities of day to day life. In this manner the dedicated *Karmayogi* moves through the various avenues of life very peacefully. The scene may change from pleasurable events to painful ones but he remains unperturbed being constantly united in the awareness of the Supreme-soul. Dr. Annie Besant in her commentary on *Bhagwad Geeta* writes : "Yogi dwells in calm and ceaseless contemplation while his body and mind are actively employed in discharging the duties that fall to his lot in life. That the spiritual man need not be a recluse, that union with divine life may be achieved and maintained in the midst of worldly affairs, that the obstacles to that union lie, not outside us, but within us, such is the central lesson of the *Bhagawad Geeta*".

Throughout the long dialogue Sri Kṛṣṇa counsels Arjuna with love and patience. He educates him step by step about the concept of *Dharma* and liberates him from the conditioned self-created limitations. Towards the end, He asks Arjuna, whether his questions have been answered appropriately or not—Arjuna's answer comes very naturally and spontaneously, "O'Krsna my ignorance is destroyed, now I feel stable and integrated". Arjuna's reply indicates his psychological transformation and inner stability. He feels awakened to the consciousness of the Supreme indwelling Divinity and takes refuge in Lord with faith, willingness and acceptance. He feels introduced to a higher truth wherein his memory returns with a new concept of truth and *swadharma*. He comprehends the essentiality of his nature and re-evaluates the entire situation in an enlightened state of mind. The concept of *Dharma* becomes very clear to him. All the mixed concepts of *Dharma* and his self-assumed notions about obligations and duties start blending into one essential *Dharma*—accept to live in the consciousness of the presence of the Supreme Divinity and experience one's own immortality. Throughout the dramatic psychological change in Arjuna, Sri Kṛṣṇa remains alert about the deep-rooted conflict of His dear friend and makes use of the most appropriate words in His answers to Arjuna's questions.

Revelation of this magnanimity is indeed the prerogative of each and every individual. This rediscovery of one's own essential nature is possible for every one, only if the person surrenders himself to the grace of the indweller. The grace of the Supreme Lord lies perpetually within the various sheaths of one's own awareness. It lies veiled beneath one's own individualized ego-centric self; so when a person takes refuge in God the purity and essentiality of his own Divine nature unfolds itself and becomes available to him. Arjuna's experience of grace indicates his feeling of inner peace and stability in contrast to the turmoil of previous emotions. He feels stabilized, confident, integrated, firm and enthusiastic about performing his duty.

Performance of action is only a medium for the revelation of the Divine power and yogic unity. Excellence in the performance of action lies in direct proportion to the connectedness of the individual to the source of life. The person who resorts to yogic unity of the Supreme-Soul and performs all his work with the guidance of the infinite Divinity he is rewarded with excellence in work and liberation in life here and hereafter. The concluding word of the dialogue is *mama* while the opening word has been *Dharma*. The entire message of *Geeta* is enclosed in these two words—*mama dharma*—means *my dharma*. The life on earth becomes peaceful, productive, creative, prosperous and instrumental for liberation only if a person could understand the meaning of—*my dharma*. *Dharma* of every individual is to remain united with the indwelling Divinity and perform all the activities of life in perfect harmony with the voice of the Supreme-Self.

Sri Kṛṣṇa makes it very clear to Arjuna that *mukti* or *mokṣa* is not only at departure from the world. Liberation and absolute Bliss can be achieved in one's present life-time and also in the life hereafter. Liberation is in living in the awareness of the Divine, liberation is the acceptance of the self, liberation is living a life above the dualities such as pleasure and pain, gain and loss, honour and dishonour, victory and defeat. Liberation is living in the nature of the Supreme Soul. *Mokṣa* or *Nirvāṇa* is right here in the middle of *Samsāra*. It is to be in touch with the centre of our being—*sahaja avasthā,* where we are not compelled by our ego-centric conditioned habits, where we have no regrets, no expectations, no fear and we can hold on to our essential nature which is pure, peaceful and absolute Bliss.

The message of Sri Kṛṣṇa summarizes the essential teachings of the ancient scriptures and is addressed to the entire mankind. This is the gospel of ardent devotion to the Lord combined with proper performance of action in the mundane world. The path of complete devotion and dedication has been evaluated to be the highest. The message illustrates the majesty of the yogic unity with sincere devotion, which makes possible to live a life totally grounded in the consciousness of the Lord, while being engaged in activities of the world. It reconciles the *yoga* of knowledge, devotion and action into one—*yoga* of total surrender in God. Asceticism, without knowledge of the Self is impossible, and the knowledge of the Self and the knowledge of the *Karmayoga* is possible only with total surrender in God. Living a life in the consciousness of the Supreme Lord and to perform all duties of the world in the consciousness of the Divine, is the gateway to freedom in life here and hereafter. In the words of Dr. Franklin Edgerton, the professor of Sanskrit and comparative philosophy in Yale University: *"Geeta's* religion is a compromise between the speculation of the intellectuals and the emotionalism of popular religion. So the notion of *bhakti,* devotion, enters into its scheme of salvation by a side-door, without at first displacing the old intellectual theory of salvation by knowledge. At least it is rationalized in this way. It is represented that by devoted love of God one can attain knowledge (of God), and so indirectly the salvation which comes through this knowledge."

It is indeed so true that there is no other book so inspiring, so enlightening, so refreshing, so absorbing in which the understanding of the Self is renewed every time we read. It presents the most wonderful guidance for self-realization and God-realization. Throughout the dialogue there is not a single *shloka* (verse) which lacks interest and not a single one, any one would like to skip. There is special emphasis on the transcendental remoteness of the Divine as well as the loving intimacy of the Lord. The presence of Sri Kṛṣṇa is felt and perceived behind His words. Throughout the dialogue one perceives the subtle gleam of Divinity and the spiritual mystery of Lord Kṛṣṇa—as God incarnate, the protector of *Dharma* (righteousness) the compassionate and caring friend of Arjuna, the speaker of the holy sermon and the greatest teacher of the world. This mesmeric touch of the Lord makes the dialogue simply unique. The message of *Bhagawad Geeta,* has been held in deep reverence by the sages, philosophers and learned scholars all over the world. It is a comprehensive treatise of universal religion, a compendium of spiritual wisdom and the most appropriate guide for living a life in peace, harmony, mutual love and freedom. It is one of the most well-known and revered religious texts, among the other scriptures of the world. In the words of Barbara Stoler Miller, "the dramatic moral crisis that is central to the *Bhagawad Geeta* has inspired centuries of Indian philosophers and practical men of wisdom, as well as Western thinkers such as Thoreau, Emerson and Eliot. Interpretations of the *Geeta,* as it is commonly referred to in India, are as varied as the figures who have commented on it. From Shankara, the great Hindu philosopher of the eighth century, to Mahatma Gandhi, the leader of India's independence struggle in the twentieth century, each thinker has emphasized the path to spiritual liberation that suited to his view of reality. These interpretations reflect the intentionally multifaceted message of Sri Kṛṣṇa's teaching". There are hundreds of translations of *Bhagawad Geeta* both in Indian and in many foreign languages. This is perhaps the most widely translated scripture of the world. In the words of Dr. Radhakrishnan, "for centuries people have found comfort in this great book which sets forth in precise and penetrating words the essential principles of a spiritual religion which are not contingent on ill-founded facts, unscientific dogmas or arbitrary fancies. With long history of spiritual power, it serves even today as a light to all who will receive illumination from the profundity of its wisdom which insists on a world wider and deeper than wars and revolutions can touch. It is a powerful shaping factor in the renewal of spiritual life and has secured an assured place among the world's greatest scriptures." Ever since the teachings of *Geeta* have become known to the people in Europe and America it has quickly won the interest and admiration of millions. Many philosophical and religious groups in foreign countries hold the same respect for *Geeta* as the people in India. The well-known professor of religion in Oxford University, Dr. Zaehner, has written about the glory of the sacred song in these words, "*Geeta* is a first-hand guide to the ancient roots of Vedic religion. Although in *Śvetāsvatara Upaniṣad* the transcendence of the personal God has been affirmed to some extent—with *Geeta* came the devotional religion". The great respect and appreciation for *Geeta* has been voiced by Warren Hastings, the first British Governor General of India in year 1773. He has said, "when the British Empire is lost in oblivion, when its sources of wealth and prosperity are not remembered, this scripture and lesson it contains will continue to inspire millions of people in this world". Sir Edwin Arnold has designated the holy *Geeta* to be the incomparable religious classic of India. He writes: "in plain but noble language it unfolds its philosophical system which remains to this day the Brahmanic belief blending as it does the doctrines of Kapila, Patañjalī and the *Vedas.* So lofty are many of its declarations, so sublime its aspirations, so pure and tender its piety." He further writes: "English literature would be certainly incomplete without possessing in popular form, a poetical and philosophical work so dear to India." Dr. Annie Besant re-echoes this revered tribute in these words, "among the priceless teachings that may be found in the great Hindu poem of the *Mahabharata,* there is none so rare and precious as this The Lord's song". Dr. Barbara Stoler Miller, in her translation of *Bhagawad Geeta* mentions about the fascination of Thoreau and Emerson for the holy dialogue and why did Henry David Thoreau take the *Bhagawad Geeta* to Walden Pond? She writes "among the many works of Asian literature that were studied in Concord, Massachusetts, in the mid-nineteenth century, none was more influential than the *Bhagawad Geeta*". She quotes the profound response of Thoreau to the study of the Holy sermon in these words, "in the morning I bathe my intellect in the stupendous and cosmogonal philosophy of the *Bhagawad Geeta,* since whose composition years of the gods have elapsed, and in comparison with which our modern world and its literature seem puny and trivial." She has also quoted some beautiful lines from one of the journals of Ralph Waldo Emerson, "It was the first of books; it was as if an empire spoke to us, nothing small or unworthy but large, serene, consistent, the voice of an old intelligence which in another age and climate had pondered and thus disposed of the same questions which exercise us".

The most ancient translation of *Bhagawad Geeta* was by Sri Shankaracharya in 800 A.D. which refers to many previous ones, written in the past by other seers and sages. Other well-known translations have been by Sri Ramanuja in the eleventh century and by Sri Madhavacharya in the 13th century and also by Sridhara and Sri Jnaneshwarji. The holy *Geeta* has been translated into English and so many other languages, the first English translation was published by Charles Wilkins in the year 1785. *Geeta* has been translated into Latin by Lassen, into Greek by Galanos, into Italian by Stanislov Gatti, into French by Burnouf, into English by Thompson, Davis, Dr. Annie Besant, Edwin Arnold, Dr. Franklin Edgerton, Dr. Zaehner, Dr. Barabara Stoler Miller, Stephen Mitchell, Aldous Huxley, Charles Wilkins and Brook; into German by Maxmuller and J.W. Hauer, a Sanskrit scholar, who has upheld *Bhagawad Geeta* to be the most respectable scriptural text in the religious faith of people in Germany. He has designated *Geeta* to be the great work of imperishable significance. There are hundreds of other translations of *Bhagawad Geeta* by great Indian Scholars. The most well-known of the modern time are by Sri Bal Gangadhar Tilak, Ari Aurobindo, Mahatma Gandhi, Swami Sivananda, Jayadayal Goyendka, Swami Tapasayananda, Swami Chidbavananda,

Swami Vivekananda, Maharishi Mahesh Yogi, Sri Ramsukdhas, Sri Vinobhaji, Swami Chinmayananda, Swami Rama, Swami Prabhupada, Dr. S. Radhakrishnan, and Sri Satwalekar. Among the Persian writers the famous translations of *Bhagawad Geeta* has been done by Darashikoh and Khwaja Dil Mohammed. All of these are worthy of great respect, veneration and appreciation.

The present translation is only a humble addition to the work, which has been accomplished earlier by the learned *Geeta* scholars. This pocket edition with comprehensive introduction has been brought out in order to encourage the modern generation in the study of this great ancient scripture. The entire purpose of composing this pocket book in simple language is to pass on the wisdom of the ages to the coming generations. The great sages recommend that every body should always keep the small edition of Geeta in his pocket for the study of selected verses whenever there is an opportunity. This helps the person to be in harmony with the voice of God and receive sufficient guidance in the activities of day-to-day life. The regular study of holy *Geeta* makes us receptive to the call of the Divine and helps us to become introduced to our own self and rediscover the missing alignment within our own personality which brings freedom in due course of time. The message of the holy dialogue is indeed phenomenal—the gateway to peace, happiness, harmony and freedom.

April, 2002 —*Prabha Duneja*

Chapter One

VISHĀDAYOGA

THE YOGA OF THE DESPONDENCY OF ARJUNA

Dhṛtarāstra Uvāca :

dharmakṣetre kurukṣetre samavetā yuyutsavaḥ

māmakāḥ pāṇḍavāścaiva kimakurvata sañjaya ||1||

Dhṛtarāṣtra said :

(1) On the holy field of Kurukshetra, assembled together and eager to fight the battle, what did my sons and the sons of Pandu do?, O'Sanjaya.

Sañjaya Uvāca :

dṛṣṭvā tu pāṇḍavānīkaṁ vyūḍhaṁ duryodhanastadā

ācāryamupasaṅgamya rājā vacanamabravīṭ ||2||

Sañjaya said :

(2) Having seen the army of the Pandavas arrayed in the battle, Prince Duryodhana then approached his teacher Dronacharya, and spoke

these words.

paśyaitāṁ pāṇḍuputrāṇāmācārya mahatīṁ camūm
vyūḍhāṁ drupadaputreṇa tava śiṣyeṇa dhīmatā ||3||

(3) Behold O' Teacher, this mighty army of the sons of Pandu, arrayed by the son of King Drupada, thy wise disciple.

atra śūrā maheṣvāsā bhīmārjunasamā yudhi
yuyudhāno virāṭaśca drupadaśca mahārathaḥ ||4||
dhṛṣṭaketuścekitānaḥ kāśirājaśca vīryavān
purujitkuntibhojaśca śaibyaśca narapuṅgavaḥ ||5||
yudhāmanyuśca vikrānta uttamaujāśca vīryavān
saubhadro draupadeyāśca sarva eva mahārathāḥ ||6||

(4, 5, 6) Here are the heroes, the mighty archers, who are equal in warfare to Bhima and Arjuna—Yuyudhana, Virata and the great chariot-warrior Drupada. Dhristaketu, Cekitana, and the valiant King of Kasi; Purujit, Kuntibhoja, and Saibya, the best among men; the mighty Yudhamanyu, the valiant Uttamauja, Abhimanyu, the son of Subhadra and the five sons of Draupadi are also there. All of them are the well-known chariot-warriors.

asmākaṁ tu viśiṣṭā ye tānnibodha dvijottama
nāyakā mama sainyasya sañjñārthaṁ tānbravīmi te ||7||

(7) Know also O'noblest of the twice-born! the distinguished warriors of our side, the generals of my army. I will name them for your information.

bhavānbhīṣmaśca karṇaśca kṛpaśca samitiñjayaḥ
aśvatthāmā vikarṇaśca saumadattistathaiva ca ||8||

(8) Yourself and Bhishma, Karna and also Kripa who is ever victorious in battle; Ashwatthama, Vikarna and Saumadatti, the son of Somadatta.

anye ca bahavaḥ śūrā madarthe tyaktajīvitāḥ
nānāśastraprahraṇāḥ sarve yuddhaviśāradāḥ ||9||

(9) And there are many other heroes, who are ready to give up their lives for my sake; they are equipped with many kinds of weapons and all of them are skilled in the strategy of warfare.

aparyāptaṁ tadasmākaṁ balaṁ bhīṣmābhirakṣitam
paryāptaṁ tvidameteṣāṁ balaṁ bhīmābhirakṣitam ||10||

(10) This army of ours, which is guarded and marshalled by Bhishma, is insufficient; while their army, which is marshalled by Bhima is sufficient.

ayaneṣu ca sarveṣu yathābhāgamavasthitāḥ
bhīṣmamevā'bhirakṣantu bhavantaḥ sarva eva hi ||11||

(11) Therefore, all of you, stationed in your respective positions, in every division, must guard Bhishma in particular by all means.

tasya sañjanayanharṣaṁ kuruvṛddhaḥ pitāmahaḥ

siṁhanādaṁ vinadyoccaiḥ śaṅkhaṁ dadhmau pratāpavān ||12||

(12) Then the revered grandsire Bhishma the oldest of the Kauravas roaring like a lion, blew his conch in order to cheer up Duryodhana.

tataḥ śaṅkhāśca bheryaśca paṇavānakagomukhāḥ

sahasaivābhyahanyanta sa śabdastumulo'bhavat ||13||

(13) Then conches, kettledrums, tabors, drums and cow-horns blared forth all at once and the noise became tumultuous.

tataḥ śvetairhayairyukte mahati syandane sthitau

mādhavaḥ pāṇḍvaścaiva divyau śaṅkhau pradadhmatuḥ ||14||

(14) Then seated in the magnificent chariot, yoked with white horses, Srī Kṛṣṇa as well as Arjuna blew their celestial conches.

pāñcajanyaṁ hṛṣīkeśo devadattaṁ dhanañjayaḥ

pauṇḍraṁ dadhmau mahāśaṅkhaṁ bhīmakarmā vṛkodaraḥ ||15||

(15) Srī Kṛṣṇa blew His conch named Panchajanya, and Arjuna blew his conch called Devadatta, while Bhima the doer of terrific deeds blew his mighty conch, Paundra.

anantavijayaṁ rājā kuntīputro yudhiṣṭhiraḥ

nakulaḥ sahadevaśca sughoṣamaṇipuṣpakau ||16||

(16) The King Yudhisthira, the son of Kunti, blew his conch Anantavijaya and Nakula and Sahadeva blew their respective conches, the Sughosa and the Manipuspaka.

kāśyaśca parameṣvāsaḥ śikhaṇḍī ca mahārathaḥ
dhṛṣṭadyumno virāṭaśca sātyakiścāparājitaḥ ||17||
drupado draupadeyāśca sarvaśaḥ pṛthivīpate
saubhadraśca mahābāhuḥ śaṅkhāndadhamuḥ pṛthak-pṛthak ||18||

(17, 18) The King of Kasi, an excellent archer; Sikhandi, the great chariot-warrior, Dhristadyumna and Virata and the invincible Satyaki, the King Drupada as well as the five sons of Draupadi and the mighty-armed Abhimanyu, the son of Subhadra, every one of them blew their respective conches.

sa ghoṣo dhārtarāṣṭrāṇāṁ hṛdayāni vyadārayat
nabhaśca pṛthivīṁ caiva tumulo vyanunādayan ||19||

(19) The tumultuous uproar has pierced the hearts of Dhritrashtra's sons resounding through the heaven and the earth.

atha vyavasthitāndṛṣṭvā dhārtarāṣṭrān kapidhvajaḥ
pravṛtte śastrasampāte dhanurudyamya pāṇḍavaḥ ||20||
hṛṣīkeśaṁ tadā vākyamidamāha mahīpate

(20, 21) Then looking at the people of Dhritrashtra's sons, standing arrayed in battle and about to commence with their weapons; Arjuna, the son of Pandu, whose flag ensign was monkey, he lifted his bow and said the following words to the Lord of the earth.

Arjuna Uvāca :

senayorubhayormadhye rathaṁ sthāpaya me'cyuta ||21||

yāvadetānnirīkṣe'haṁ yoddhukāmānavasthitān

kairmayā saha yoddhavyam-asminraṇasamudyame ||22||

Arjuna said :

(21, 22) O'Achyuta (Srī Kṛṣṇa)! Please place my chariot between the two armies, so that I may see all those, who stand here desirous of war with whom I have to fight this battle.

yotsyamānānavekṣehaṁ ya ete'tra samāgatāḥ

dhārtarāṣṭrasya durbuddher-yuddhe priyacikīrṣavaḥ ||23||

(23) I want to see those who are assembled here with an intent to fight and are desirous to please in battle, the evil minded son of Dhritrashtra (Duryodhana).

Sañjaya Uvāca :

evamukto hṛṣīkeśo guḍākeśena bhārata

senayorubhayormadhye sthāpayitvā rathottamam ||24||

bhīṣmadroṇapramukhataḥ sarveṣāṁ ca mahīkṣitām
uvāca pārtha paśyaitān samavetānkurūniti ||25||

Sanjaya said :

(24, 25) O'descendant of Bharata (Dhritrashtra), thus addressed by Gudakesa (Arjuna), Hrishikesha (Srī Kṛṣṇa) having placed the magnificent chariot in the middle of the two armies; in front of Bhisma and Drona and all the other kings said, "O'Arjuna, behold these Kurus assembled here."

tatrāpaśyat sthitānpārthaḥ pitṛnatha pitāmahān
ācāryānmātulānbhrātṛnputrānpautrānsakhīṅstathā ||26||
śvasurānsuhṛdaścaiva senayorubhayorapi

(26) There, Arjuna beholds, stationed between both the armies; his uncles, granduncles, teachers, maternal uncles, brothers, cousins, sons, grandsons, fathers-in-law and friends as well.

tānsamīkṣya sa kaunteyaḥ sarvānbandhūnavasthitān ||27||
kṛpayā parayāviṣṭo viṣīdannidamabravīt

(27) Looking at all the kinsmen, thus assembled there, Arjuna feels overwhelmed with deep compassion and speaks these words.

Arjuna Uvāca :

dṛṣṭvemaṁ svajanaṁ kṛṣṇa yuyutsuṁ samupasthitam ||28||

sīdanti mama gātrāṇi mukhaṁ ca pariśuṣyati

vepathuśca śarīre me romaharṣaśca jāyate ||29||

gāṇḍīvaṁ sraṅsate hastāt tvakcaiva paridahyate

na ca śaknomyavasthātuṁ bhramatīva ca me manaḥ ||30||

Arjuna said :

(28, 29, 30) O'Kṛṣṇa, at the sight of these kinsmen, thus arrayed here, eager for battle, my limbs have become feeble and my mouth is parched, my whole body quivers and my hair stand on end. The Gandiva is slipping from my hands and my skin is burning all over. I am not able to stand firmly and my mind seems to reel.

nimittāni ca paśyāmi viparītāni keśava

na ca śreyo'nupaśyāmi hatvā svajanamāhave ||31||

(31) And I see very inauspicious omens, O'Kesava (Srī Kṛṣṇa); I do not perceive any good in killing my kinsmen in the battle.

na kāṅkṣe vijayaṁ kṛṣṇa na ca rājyaṁ sukhāni ca

kiṁ no rājyena govinda kiṁ bhogairjīvitena vā ||32||

(32) O'Kṛṣṇa, I do not desire any victory, nor kingdom, nor pleasures. What is the use of kingdom to us, O'Govinda, or the luxuries or even life itself.

yeṣāmarthe kāṅkṣitaṁ no rājyaṁ bhogāḥ sukhāni ca
ta ime'vasthitā yuddhe prāṇāṅstyaktvā dhanāni ca ||33||

(33) Those, for whose sake we desire kingdom, enjoyments and pleasures, are standing poised for battle and ready to give up their lives and wealth.

ācāryāḥ pitaraḥ putrāstathaiva ca pitāmahāḥ
mātulāḥ śvaśurāḥ pautrāḥ śyālāḥ sambandhinastathā ||34||

(34) The teachers, uncles, sons and grandfathers, maternal uncles, fathers-in-law, grandsons, brothers-in-law, and other relatives as well.

etānna hantumicchāmi ghnato'pi madhusūdana
api trailokyarājyasya hetoḥ kim nu mahīkṛte ||35||

(35) These, I do not want to kill, even though they may kill me, O'Slayer of Madhu (Kṛṣṇa); even for the sovereignty of the three worlds—how then just for the sake of the earthly lordship?

nihatya dhārtarāṣṭrānnaḥ kā prītiḥ syājjanārdana
pāpamevāśrayedasmānhatvaitānātatāyinaḥ ||36||

(36) By killing the sons of Dhritrashtra, what pleasure can be ours, O' Kṛṣṇa? Only the sin will accrue to us by slaying these desperadoes.

tasmānnārhā vayaṁ hantuṁ dhārtarāṣṭrān svabāndhavān
svajanaṁ hi kathaṁ hatvā sukhinaḥ syāma mādhava ||37||

(37) Therefore, it is not appropriate for us to kill our relatives, the sons of Dhritrashtra. For, if we kill our kinsmen, how can we be happy, O' Madhva (Kṛṣṇa)?

yadyapyete na paśyanti lobhopahatacetasaḥ
kulakṣayakṛtaṁ doṣaṁ mitradrohe ca pātakam ||38||
kathaṁ na jñeyamasmābhiḥ pāpādasmānnivartitum
kulakṣayakṛtaṁ doṣaṁ prapaśyadbhirjanārdana ||39||

(38, 39) Although these people, whose minds are blinded by greed, do not perceive evil in the destruction of their own race, and the sin, in treachery to friends; why shouldn't we have the wisdom to turn away from this crime, we can clearly see the sin which is involved in the destruction of the family, O'Janardana (Kṛṣṇa)?

kulakṣaye praṇaśyanti kuladharmāḥ sanātanāḥ
dharme naṣṭe kulaṁ kṛtsnamadharmo'bhibhavatyuta ||40||

(40) With the destruction of a family, the ancient religious traditions are destroyed; with the disappearance of the religious traditions, the unrighteousness takes hold of the entire family.

adharmābhibhavātkṛṣṇa praduṣyanti kulastriyaḥ
strīṣu duṣṭāsu vārṣṇeya jāyate varṇasaṅkaraḥ ||41||

(41) With the prevalence of unrighteousness, O'Kṛṣṇa, the women of the family become corrupt; when the women become corrupt, O'Varsneya (Kṛṣṇa) there arise the intermixture of castes.

saṇkaro narakāyaiva kulaghnānāṁ kulasya ca
patanti pitaro hyeṣāṁ luptapiṇḍodakakriyāḥ ||42||

(42) The confusion of castes leads to hell the entire clan itself and its destroyers; for the spirits of the ancestors fall, deprived of their offerings of rice and water.

doṣairetaiḥ kulaghnānāṁ varṇasaṅkarakārakaiḥ
utsādyante jātidharmāḥ kuladharmāśca śāśvatāḥ ||43||

(43) By these evil deeds of the destroyers of the family which create confusion of Varnas, the ancient laws of the caste and family are destroyed.

utsannakuladharmāṇāṁ manuṣyāṇāṁ janārdana
narake'niyataṁ vāso bhavatītyanuśuśruma ||44||

(44) For those men, in whose families, the ancient religious traditions are destroyed, a place in hell is ordained, O'Kṛṣṇa, we have heard it so.

aho bata mahatpāpaṁ kartuṁ vyavasitā vayam
yadrājyasukhalobhena hantuṁ svajanamudyatāḥ ||45||

(45) Alas! We have resolved to commit a great

sin in which we are prepared to kill our own kinsmen, merely out of our desire for sovereignty and enjoyments.

yadi māmpratīkāramaśastraṁ śastrapāṇayaḥ
dhārtarāṣṭrā raṇe hanyustanme kṣemataraṁ bhavet ||46||

(46) It will be better for me if the well-armed sons of Dhritrashtra do kill me in the battle, while I am unarmed and unresisting.

Sañjaya Uvāca :

evamuktvārjunaḥ saṅkhye rathopastha upāviśat
visṛjya saśaraṁ cāpaṁ śokasaṁvignamānasaḥ ||47||

Sañjaya said :

(47) Having spoken thus, in the middle of the battlefield, Arjuna puts away his bow and arrows and sinks down on the seat of his chariot, with his mind overwhelmed with grief.

'AUM TAT SAT'—Thus, in the Upanishad of the glorious Bhagawad Geeta, the science of the Brahman (Absolute) the scripture of yoga, the dialogue between Srī Kṛṣṇa and Arjuna—thus, ends the chapter one entitled "Viśādyoga".

Chapter Two

SĀMKHYAYOGA

THE YOGA OF TRANSCENDENTAL KNOWLEDGE

Sañjaya Uvāca :

taṁ tathā kṛpayāviṣṭamaśrupūrṇākulekṣaṇam
viṣīdantamidaṁ vākyamuvāca madhusūdanaḥ ||1||

Sañjaya said :

(1) To him, who was thus overwhelmed with pity, whose eyes were filled with tears and was agitated, Madhusudana (Srī Kṛṣṇa) spoke these words.

Śrī Bhagavānuvāca :

kutastvā kaśmalamidaṁ viṣame samupasthitam
anāryajuṣṭamasvargyamakīrtikaramarjuna ||2||

The Blessed Lord said :

(2) From where has come to you this despondency, O'Arjuna in this hour of crisis? It is unfit for a noble man and is indeed very

disgraceful. It neither leads to heaven nor to any worldly fame and glory.

klaibyaṁ mā sma gamaḥ pārtha naitattvayyupapadyate
kṣudraṁ hṛdayadaurbalyaṁ tyaktvottiṣṭha parantapa ||3||

(3) Yield not to this unmanliness, O'Arjuna. It does not befit you. Shake off this petty faint-heartedness and stand up, O'Scorcher of the enemies.

Arjuna Uvāca :

kathaṁ bhīṣmamahaṁ saṅkhye droṇaṁ ca madhusūdana
iṣubhiḥ pratiyotsyāmi pūjārhāvarisūdana ||4||

Arjuna said :

(4) O'Kṛṣṇa, how can I fight in the battle with arrows against Bhishma and Drona? They are worthy of my respect and reverence, O'destroyer of the foes.

gurūnahatvā hi mahānubhāvān
śreyo bhoktuṁ bhaikṣyamapīḥ loke
hatvārthakāmānstu gurūnihaiva
bhuṇjīya bhogān rudhirapradigdhān ||5||

(5) It is better to live on alms in this world than to slay these venerable teachers, because even after killing them we will enjoy only bloodstained

wealth, pleasure and worldly enjoyment.

na caitadvidmaḥ kataranno garīyo
yadvā jayema yadi vā no jayeyuḥ
yāneva hatvā na jijīviṣāma-
ste'vasthitāḥ pramukhe dhārtarāṣṭrāḥ ||6||

(6) We do not know which is better, whether we should conquer them or they should conquer us. The sons of Dhritarastra, by killing whom, we don't even wish to live, are arrayed against us.

kārpaṇyadoṣopahatasvabhāvaḥ
pṛcchāmi tvāṁ dharmasammūḍhacetāḥ
yacchreyaḥ syānniścitaṁ brūhi tanme
śiṣyaste'haṁ śādhi māṁ tvāṁ prapannam ||7||

(7) My heart is overpowered by the weakness of pity and my mind is confused about my duty; I request Thee, to tell me for certain, which is decidedly good for me. I am your disciple. Teach me, who has taken refuge in You.

na hi prapaśyāmi mamāpanudyād
yacchokamucchoṣaṇamindriyāṇām
avāpya bhūmāvasapatnamṛddhaṁ
rājyaṁ surāṇāmapi cādhipatyam ||8||

(8) I don't see any means, that can dispel this

grief which is drying up my senses; even if I attain undisputed sovereignty and an affluent kingdom on this earth or even the Lordship over the gods.

Sañjaya Uvāca :

evamuktvā hṛṣīkeśaṁ guḍākeśaḥ parantapa

na yotsya iti govindamuktvā tūṣṇīṁ babhūva ha ||9||

Sañjaya said :

(9) Having thus spoken to Srī Kṛṣṇa, Arjuna the conqueror of sleep and the destroyer of foes said "I will not fight" and became silent.

tamuvāca hṛṣīkeśaḥ prahasanniva bhārata

senayorubhayormadhye viṣīdantamidaṁ vacaḥ ||10||

(10) Then, O' Dhritarastra, to him who was despondent in the midst of the two armies, Srī Kṛṣṇa spoke the following words with a smile on His face.

Śrī Bhagavānuvāca :

aśocyānanvaśocastvaṁ prajñāvādānśca bhāṣase

gatāsūnagatāsūnśca nānuśocanti paṇḍitāḥ ||11||

The Blessed Lord said :

(11) O' Arjuna, you grieve for those who should not be grieved for; yet you speak the words of wisdom. The wise men do not grieve for the

dead or for the living.

na tvevāhaṁ jātu nāsaṁ na tvaṁ neme janādhipāḥ

na caiva na bhaviṣyāmaḥ sarve vayamataḥ param ||12||

(12) There was never a time when I or you or these rulers of men did not exist; nor will there be any time in future when all of us shall cease to be.

dehino'sminyathā dehe kaumāraṁ yauvanaṁ jarā

tathā dehāntaraprāptirdhīrastatra na muhyati ||13||

(13) Just as in this body, the embodied-soul, passes through childhood, youth and old age; so too it passes into another body. The man of integral wisdom is not deluded by this.

mātrāsparśāstu kaunteya śītoṣṇasukhaduḥkhadāḥ

āgamāpāyino'nityāstāṅstitikṣasva bhārata ||14||

(14) The contact of the senses with their objects, gives rise to the feeling of cold and heat, pleasure and pain, etc., these are transitory and fleeting. Therefore learn to endure them patiently, O'Arjuna.

yaṁ hi na vyathayantyete puruṣaṁ puruṣarṣabha

samaduḥkhasukhaṁ dhīraṁ so'mṛtatvāya kalpate ||15||

(15) The man who is not tormented by these, O'Arjuna, to whom the pleasure and pain are

alike—that steadfast man becomes eligible for immortality.

nāsato vidyate bhāvo nābhāvo vidyate sataḥ
ubhayorapi dṛṣṭo'ntastvanayostattvadarśibhiḥ ||16||

(16) The unreal has no existence and the real never ceases to be; the essential truth about both of these, is perceived by the seers of truth.

avināśi tu tadviddhi yena sarvamidaṁ tatam
vināśamavyayasyāsya na kaścitkartumarhati ||17||

(17) Know that to be imperishable by which all this is pervaded. No one can bring about the destruction of the indestructible.

antavanta ime dehā nityasyoktāḥ śarīriṇaḥ
anāśino'prameyasya tasmādyudhyasva bhārata ||18||

(18) These bodies of the embodied-self are perishable while the Self is eternal, imperishable and incomprehensible. Therefore O'Arjuna, fight the battle.

ya enaṁ vetti hantāraṁ yaścainaṁ manyate hatam
ubhau tau na vijānīto nāyaṁ hanti na hanyate ||19||

(19) He who considers the soul to be the slayer and who thinks that this is slain; both of them fail to perceive the truth. The soul neither slays nor is slain.

na jāyate mriyate vā kadācinnāyaṁ
bhūtvā bhavitā vā na bhūyaḥ
ajo nityaḥ śāśvato'yaṁ purāṇo
na hanyate hanyamāne śarīre ||20||

(20) The soul is neither born nor does it ever die; having come into being once, it never ceases to be. It is unborn, eternal, permanent and primeval. It is not killed even when the body is killed.

vedāvināśinaṁ nityaṁ ya enamajamavyayam
kathaṁ sa puruṣaḥ pārtha kaṁ ghātayati hanti kam ||21||

(21) He who knows the soul to be indestructible, unborn, unchanging and immutable; how can such a person slay anyone, O'Arjuna or cause any one to slay?

vāsāṅsi jīrṇāni yathā vihāya navāni gṛhṇāti naro'parāṇi
tathā śarīrāṇi vihāya jīrṇānyanyāni saṁyāti navāni dehī ||22||

(22) As a person casts off the worn-out garments and puts on the new ones; likewise the embodied-soul discards the worn out bodies and enters into the new ones.

nainaṁ chindanti śastrāṇi nainaṁ dahati pāvakaḥ
na cainaṁ kledayantyāpo na śoṣayati mārutaḥ ||23||

(23) Weapons cannot cut the soul, nor can fire burn it. Water can not wet it nor wind can make it dry.

acchedyo'yamadāhyo'yamakledyo'śoṣya eva ca

nityaḥ sarvagataḥ sthāṇuracalo'yaṁ sanātanaḥ ||24||

(24) The soul is uncleavable and incombustible. It can be neither wetted nor dried. It is eternal, all-pervading, unchanging, immovable and primordial.

avyakto'yamacintyo'yamavikāryo'yamucyate

tasmādevaṁ viditvai'naṁ nānuśocitumarhasi ||25||

(25) This (soul) is said to be unmanifest, unthinkable and unchanging. Therefore, knowing it as such, you should not grieve.

atha cainaṁ nityajātaṁ nityaṁ vā manyase mṛtam

tathāpi tvaṁ mahābāho naivaṁ śocitumarhasi ||26||

(26) Even if you regard the soul as being continually taking birth and continually dying; even then, O'Arjuna, you should not grieve.

jātasya hi dhruvo mṛtyurdhruvaṁ janma mṛtasya ca

tasmādaparihārye'rthe na tvaṁ śocitumarhasi ||27||

(27) For, death is certain of the one who is born, and also the rebirth is certain of the one who is dead; therefore you should not grieve over

the inevitable.

avyaktādīni bhūtāni vyaktamadhyāni bhārata

avyaktanidhnānyeva tatra kā paridevanā ||28||

(28) O'Arjuna, all the beings are unmanifest in their beginnings, they become manifested in the middle state and unmanifested again in the end. What is there in this, for lamentation?

āścaryavatpaśyati kaścidena

māścaryavadvadati tathaiva cānyaḥ

āścaryavacainamanyaḥ śṛṇoti

śrutvāpyenaṁ veda na caiva kaścit ||29||

(29) One perceives the soul in great wonder, likewise another speaks of it in wonder; still another hears of it in great wonder; and even after hearing of it, hardly any one understands it.

dehī nityamavadhyo'yaṁ dehe sarvasya bhārata

tasmātsarvāṇi bhūtāni na tvaṁ śocitumarhasi ||30||

(30) O'Arjuna, the soul dwelling in the body of every one is eternal and indestructible. Therefore, you should not grieve for any creature.

svadharmamapi cāvekṣya na vikampitumarhasi

dharmyāddhi yuddhācchreyo'nyat kṣatriyasya na vidyate ||31||

(31) Besides, in consideration of your own duty as well, it does not befit you to waver. For, to a

kshatriya, there is nothing else better than a righteous war.

yadṛcchayā copapannaṁ svargadvāramapāvṛtam
sukhinaḥ kṣatriyāḥ pārtha labhante yuddhamīdṛśam ||32||

(32) Happy (fortunate) are the kshatriyas, O'Arjuna, those who are called upon to fight in a battle like this, that comes of itself as an open door to the heaven.

atha cettvamimaṁ dharmyaṁ saṅgrāmaṁ na kariṣyasi
tataḥ svadharmaṁ kīrtiṁ ca hitvā pāpamavāpsyasi ||33||

(33) But, if you do not fight this righteous war, you will be turning away from your assigned duty and respectable position. You will definitely incur sin.

akīrtiṁ cāpi bhūtāni kathayiṣyanti te'vyayām
sambhāvitasya cākīrtir maraṇādatiricyate ||34||

(34) Besides, people will speak derogatory words about you; and for the one who has been always honoured—dishonour is worse than death.

bhayādraṇāduparataṁ maṁsyante tvāṁ mahārathāḥ
yeṣāṁ ca tvaṁ bahumato bhūtvā yāsyasi lāghavam ||35||

(35) The great chariot-warriors will think, that you have withdrawn from the battle in fear. Those

men, who always held you in high esteem, will also show their disrespect.

avācyavādāṅśca bahūnvadiṣyanti tavāhitāḥ
nindantastava sāmarthyaṁ tato duḥkhataraṁ nu kim ||36||

(36) Your enemies, slandering your prowess, will speak many disgraceful words. What can be more distressing than that?

hato vā prāpsyasi svargaṁ jitvā vā bhokṣyase mahīm
tasmāduttiṣṭha kaunteya yuddhāya kṛtaniścayaḥ ||37||

(37) If killed in the battle, you will attain heaven; or, if victorious you will enjoy sovereignty of the earth. Therefore, stand up O'Arjuna, resolved to fight.

sukhaduḥkhe same kṛtvā lābhālābhau jayājayau
tato yuddhāya yujyasva naivaṁ pāpamavāpsyasi ||38||

(38) Regarding alike the pleasure and pain, gain and loss, victory and defeat; get ready for the battle. Thus, you will not incur sin.

eṣā te'bhihitā sāṅkhye buddhiryoge tvimāṁ śṛṇu
buddhyā yukto yayā pārtha karmabandhaṁ prahāsyasi ||39||

(39) This which has been declared to you so far is the wisdom of the Samkhya; now listen to the wisdom, in regard to yoga (karmayoga).

Endowed with this knowledge, O'Arjuna, you will get freedom from the bondage of karma.

nehābhikramanāśo'sti pratyavāyo na vidyate
svalpamapyasya dharmasya trāyate mahato bhayāt ||40||

(40) In this, there is no loss of effort, nor is there any fear of contrary result. Even a little practice of this discipline (Dharma) protects the individual from great fear.

vyavasāyātmikā buddhirekeha kurunandana
bahuśākhā hyanantāśca buddhayo'vyavasāyinām ||41||

(41) O'Arjuna, in this path, the resolute intellect is one pointed; whereas the intellect of the irresolute is scattered in many directions and is endlessly diverse.

yāmimāṁ puṣpitāṁ vācaṁ pravadantyavipaścitaḥ
vedavādaratāḥ pārtha nānyadastīti vādinaḥ ||42||

(42) Flowery speech is uttered by the unwise, those who take delight in the eulogizing hymns of Vedas, O' Arjuna, saying, "there is nothing other than this".

kāmātmānaḥ svargaparā janmakarmaphalapradām
kriyāviśeṣabahulāṁ bhogaiśvaryagatiṁ prati ||43||

(43) Those who are obsessed by desires, who consider heaven as their Supreme goal, they are

led to new births as the result of their actions. They perform various rituals for the sake of pleasure and power.

bhogaiśvaryaprasaktānāṁ tayāpahṛtacetsām
vyavasāyātmikā buddhiḥ samādhau na vidhīyate ||44||

(44) Those who are deeply attached to pleasure and power, whose minds are carried away by such flowery speech; they are unable to develop the resolute will of a concentrated mind in meditation.

traiguṇyaviṣayā vedā nistraiguṇyo bhavārjuna
nirdvandvo nityasattvastho niryogakṣema ātmavān ||45||

(45) The subject matter that deals with the triple attributes of nature in the *Vedas,* be Thou above those three attributes, O' Arjuna. Liberate yourself from the pairs of opposites and ever abide in the Sattva. Being free from the feeling of acquisition and preservation, stay established in the Supreme-Self.

yāvānartha udapāne sarvataḥ saṁplutodake
tāvānsarveṣu vedeṣu brāhmaṇasya vijānataḥ ||46||

(46) To a knower of Brahmana, the *Vedas* are of as much use, as is a small reservoir of water in a place which is flooded with water on all sides.

karmaṇyevādhikāraste mā phaleṣu kadācana

mā karmaphalaheturbhūrmā te saṅgo'stvakarmaṇi ||47||

(47) Your right is to perform your work only and not at all to its fruit; let not the fruit of action be your motive, nor let your attachment be to inaction.

yogasthaḥ kuru karmāṇi saṅgaṁ tyaktvā dhanañjaya

siddhyasiddhyoḥ samo bhūtvā samatvaṁ yoga ucyate ||48||

(48) O' Arjuna, perform your actions, being steadfast in Yoga. Renounce all attachments and be balanced in success and failure. Evenness (equanimity) of mind is said to be Yoga.

dūreṇa hyavaraṁ karma buddhiyogāddhanañjaya

buddhau śaraṇamanviccha kṛpaṇāḥ phalahetavaḥ ||49||

(49) Action with attachment is far inferior, O' Arjuna, to that action which is performed with the Yoga of wisdom. Seek refuge in integral wisdom; for pitiful are those who crave for the fruits of their actions.

buddhiyukto jahātīha ubhe sukṛtaduṣkṛte

tasmādyogāya yujyasva yogaḥ karmasu kauśalam ||50||

(50) Endowed with wisdom, one liberates oneself in this life, from virtues and vices. Therefore devote yourself to yoga. Yoga is skill in

action.

karmajaṁ buddhiyuktā hi phalaṁ tyaktvā manīṣiṇaḥ
janmabandhavinirmuktāḥ padaṁ gacchantyanāmayam ||51||

(51) The wise sages, who are endowed with integral wisdom, having relinquished the fruits of their actions, become liberated from the bondage of rebirth. They attain the blissful Supreme state.

yadā te mohakalilaṁ buddhirvyatitarisyati
tadā gantāsi nirvedaṁ śrotavyasya śrutasya ca ||52||

(52) When your intellect will cross the mire of delusion, then you will gain the indifference to what has been heard and what is yet to be heard.

śrutivipratipannā te yadā sthāsyati niścalā
samādhāvacalā buddhistadā yogamavāpsyasi ||53||

(53) When your intellect, which is confused by hearing the conflicting doctrines, will become firm and steadfast in meditation; then you will attain the vision of the Supreme-Self in yoga.

Arjuna Uvāca :

sthitaprajñasya kā bhāṣā samādhisthasya keśava
sthitadhīḥ kiṁ prabhāṣeta kimāsīta vrajeta kim ||54||

Arjuna said :

(54) O' Kṛṣṇa—what are the marks of the man of steadfast wisdom, who is established in

transcendental meditation? How does a man of integral wisdom speak, how does he sit and how does he walk?

Śrī Bhagavānuvāca :

prajahāti yadā kāmānsarvānpārtha manogatān

ātmanyevātmanā tuṣṭaḥ sthitaprajñastadocyate ||55||

The Blessed Lord said :

(55) When a man abandons all the desires of his mind, O'Arjuna; when he feels satisfied in the Self, by the self, then he is said to be established in transcendental wisdom.

duḥkheṣvanudvignamanāḥ sukheṣu vigataspṛhaḥ

vītarāgabhayakrodhaḥ sthitdhīrmunirucyate ||56||

(56) He whose mind remains unperturbed in the midst of sorrows, who has no longing for pleasures, who is free from passion, fear and anger, he is called a sage of steadfast wisdom.

yaḥ sarvatrānabhisnehastattatprāpya śubhāśubham

nābhinandati na dveṣṭi tasya prajñā pratiṣṭhitā ||57||

(57) He, who is unattached in all respects, at receiving good or evil, who neither rejoices nor hates, he is surely settled in transcendental wisdom.

yadā saṁharate cāyaṁ kūrmo'ṅgānīva sarvaśaḥ

indriyāṇīndriyārthebhyastasya prajñā pratiṣṭhitā ||58||

(58) When like a tortoise, which withdraws its limbs from all sides (into the shell), he withdraws his senses from the objects of the senses, then his wisdom becomes firmly set.

viṣayā vinivartante nirāhārasya dehinaḥ
rasvarjaṁ raso'pyasya paraṁ dṛṣṭvā nivartate ||59||

(59) The objects of the senses, cease to exist for the man who does not enjoy them but the taste for them persists. This lingering taste also disappears for the man of steadfast mind, on seeing the Supreme.

yatato hyapi kaunteya puruṣasya vipaścitaḥ
indriyāṇi pramāthīni haranti prasbhaṁ manaḥ ||60||

(60) O' Arjuna, the turbulent senses, do forcibly carry away the mind of even a wise man, who is practising self-control.

tāni sarvāṇi saṁyamya yukta āsīta matparaḥ
vaśe hi yasyendriyāṇi tasya prajñā pratiṣṭhitā ||61||

(61) Therefore, having controlled them all, one should remain firm in Yoga, regarding Me as the Supreme; for he, whose senses are under control, he is surely settled in transcendental wisdom.

dhyāyato viṣayānpuṁsaḥ saṅgasteṣūpajāyate
saṅgātsañjāyate kāmaḥ kāmātkrodho'bhijāyate ||62||

krodhādbhavati sammohaḥ sammohātsmṛtivibhramaḥ

smṛtibhraṁśād buddhināśo buddhināśātpraṇaśyati ||63||

(62, 63) The man who broods over the objects of the senses, he develops attachment for them; from attachment springs up desire, the desire (unfulfilled) ensues anger. From anger arises delusion, from delusion the confusion of memory; from the confusion of memory the loss of reason and from the loss of reason, he goes to complete ruin.

rāgdveṣaviyuktaistu viṣayānindriyaiścaran

ātmavaśyairvidheyātmā prasādamadhigacchati ||64||

(64) But a self-controlled man who moves among the objects of the senses with his senses under control and free from attraction and repulsion; he attains serenity of mind.

prasāde sarvaduḥkhānāṁ hānirasyopajāyate

prasannacetaso hyāśu buddhiḥ paryavatiṣṭhate ||65||

(65) With the attainment of this inner serenity, all his sufferings come to an end; and soon the intellect of such a person of tranquil mind becomes firmly established in the Bliss of the deepest awareness.

nāsti buddhirayuktasya na cāyuktasya bhāvanā

na cābhāvayataḥ śāntiraśāntasya kutaḥ sukham ||66||

(66) There is no knowledge of the Self for the

one who is not united within. The transcendental meditation is not possible for the unsteady, and to the unmeditative there can be no peace. To the man who has no inner peace, how can there be happiness?

indriyāṇāṁ hi caratāṁ yanmano'nu vidhīyate
tadasya harati prajñāṁ vāyurnāvamivāmbhasi ||67||

(67) For, when the mind yields to the wandering senses, it carries away the discrimination of the man, just as the wind carries away the ship on the water.

tasmādyasya mahābāho nigṛhītāni sarvaśaḥ
indriyāṇīndriyārthebhyastasya prajñā pratiṣṭhitā ||68||

(68) Therefore, O' Arjuna, he, whose senses are withdrawn from their objects, he becomes firmly established in the transcendental wisdom.

yā niśā sarvabhūtānāṁ tasyāṁ jāgarti saṁyamī
yasyāṁ jāgrati bhūtāni sā niśā paśyato muneḥ ||69||

(69) That which is night to all beings, in that state the self-controlled man remains awake. When all beings are awake, that is the night for the muni, who sees.

āpūryamāṇamacalapratiṣṭhaṁ
samudramāpaḥ praviśanti yadvat
tadvatkāmā yaṁ praviśanti sarve
sa śāntimāpnoti na kāmakāmī ||70||

(70) As the water of the rivers enter the ocean which though full, remains undisturbed; likewise the man in whom all desires merge themselves, he attains peace, and not the one who longs after the objects of desire.

vihāya kāmānyaḥ sarvānpumāṁścarati niḥspṛhaḥ

nirmamo nirahaṅkāraḥ sa śāntimadhigacchati ||71||

(71) He who has abandoned all his desires, and moves free from attachment and without the feeling of I and Mine, he attains the Supreme peace.

eṣā brāhmī sthitiḥ pārtha naināṁ prāpya vimuhyati

sthitvāsyāmantakāle'pi brahmanirvāṇamṛcchati ||72||

(72) This is the state of transcendental unity *(brahmisthiti)* O'Arjuna. Having attained this, he overcomes the delusion. Being established in this state, even at the time of death, he attains the Supreme Blissful state (Brahma-Nirvana).

'AUM TAT SAT'—Thus, in the Upanishad of the glorious Bhagawad Geeta, the science of the Brahman (Absolute) the scripture of yoga, the dialogue between Srī Kṛṣṇa and Arjuna thus, ends the chapter two entitled "Saṁkhyayoga".

Chapter Three

THE KARMAYOGA

THE YOGA OF ACTION

Arjuna Uvāca :

jyāyasī cetkarmaṇaste matā buddhirjanārdana

tatkiṁ karmaṇi ghore māṁ niyojayasi keśava ||1||

Arjuna said :

(1) If you consider that knowledge is superior to action, O'Kṛṣṇa, then why do you ask me to engage in this terrible action?

vyāmiśreṇeva vākyena buddhiṁ mohayasīva me

tadekaṁ vada niścitya yena śreyo'hamāpnuyām ||2||

(2) With an apparently conflicting statement, you seem to confuse my mind. Therefore, please tell me decisively that 'One', by which I may attain the highest good.

Śrī Bhagavānuvāca :

loke'smindvividhā niṣṭhā purā proktā mayānagha

jñānayogena sāṅkhyānāṁ karmayogena yoginām ||3||

The Blessed Lord said :

(3) O'Arjuna, in this world a twofold path has been declared by Me earlier; the path of knowledge of the Samkhyas and the path of 'Karma-yoga' of the yogins.

na karmaṇāmanārambhānnaiṣkarmyaṁ puruṣo'śnute
na ca sannyasanādeva siddhiṁ samadhigacchati ||4||

(4) Not by abstention from work, does a man attain liberation from action; nor by mere renunciation does he attain perfection.

na hi kaścitkṣaṇamapi jātu tiṣṭhatyakarmakṛt
kāryate hyavaśaḥ karma sarvaḥ prakṛtijairguṇaiḥ ||5||

(5) For no one can remain even for a moment without performing action; everyone is made to act helplessly indeed, forced by the impulses born of nature.

karmendriyāṇi saṅyamya ya āste mansā smaran
indriyārthānvimūḍhātmā mithyācāraḥ sa ucyate ||6||

(6) He who controls his organs of actions and sits brooding over the objects of senses, he is said to be a self-deluded hypocrite.

yastvindriyāṇi manasā niyamyārabhate'rjuna
karmendriyaiḥ karmayogamasktaḥ sa viśiṣyate ||7||

(7) But, he who controls his senses by the mind, O'Arjuna, and engages himself in the

Karmayoga; with the organs of action, without any attachment—he definitely excels.

niyatam̐ kuru karma tvam̐ karma jyāyo hyakarmaṇaḥ
śarīrayātrāpi ca te na prasiddhyedkarmaṇaḥ ||8||

(8) Therefore, you must perform your assigned work, for action is superior to inaction; and even the maintenance of your physical body cannot be possible for you, without action.

yajñārthātkarmaṇo'nyatra loko'yam̐ karmabandhanaḥ
tadartham̐ karma kaunteya muktasaṅgaḥ samācara ||9||

(9) The world is bound by actions, other than those performed for the sake of sacrifice (selflessly). Therefore, O' Arjuna, perform your work for that sake alone, being free from attachment.

sahayajñāḥ prajāḥ sṛṣṭvā puro'vāca prajāpatiḥ
anena prasaviṣyadhvameṣa vo'stivaṣṭakāmadhuk ||10||

(10) At the beginning of creation the Lord of all beings created mankind along with the sacrifice and said "by this you may prosper"; let this be the milch-cow of your desires.

devānbhāvayatānena te devā bhāvayantu vaḥ
parasparam̐ bhāvayantaḥ śreyaḥ paramavāpsyatha ||11||

(11) With this, you foster the gods and may those gods foster you; thus fostering each other,

you will attain to the highest good.

iṣṭānbhogānhi vo devā dāsyante yajñabhāvitāḥ

tairdattānapradāyai'bhyo yo bhuṅkte stena eva saḥ ||12||

(12) The gods pleased (nourished) by the sacrifice will surely bestow upon you the desired enjoyments. He, who enjoys the bounties of the gods without offering them anything in return, is verily a thief.

yajñaśiṣṭāśinaḥ santo mucyante sarvakilbiṣaiḥ

bhuñjate te tvaghaṁ pāpā ye pacantyātmakāraṇāt ||13||

(13) The virtuous, who eat the remnants of the sacrifice (yajña) are released from all sins; but the wicked, who cook food only for their own sake verily eat sin.

annādbhavanti bhūtāni parjanyādannasambhavaḥ

yajñādbhavati parjanyo yajñaḥ karmasamudbhavaḥ ||14||

(14) All beings have evolved from food. The food is produced from rain, the rain ensues from sacrifice, and sacrifice is rooted in action.

karma brahmodbhavaṁ viddhi brahmākṣarasamudbhavam

tasmātsarvagataṁ brahma nityaṁ yajñe pratiṣṭhitam ||15||

(15) Know that action has its origin in Brahma and Brahma proceeds from the imperishable. Therefore, the all-pervading infinite (God) is always present in the sacrifice (yajña).

evaṁ pravartitaṁ cakraṁ nānuvartayatīha yaḥ

aghāyurindriyārāmo moghaṁ pārtha sa jīvati ||16||

(16) He who does not follow the wheel of creation thus set in motion here; leads a sinful life; rejoicing in the senses. He surely lives in vain, O'Arjuna.

yastvātmaratireva syādātmatṛptaśca mānavaḥ

ātmanyeva ca santuṣṭas tasya kāryaṁ na vidyate ||17||

(17) But the person, who delights only in the Self, who remains satisfied in the consciousness of the Self and is contented in the Self alone; for him there is nothing to be done.

naiva tasya kṛtenārtho nākṛteneha kaścana

na cāsya sarvabhūteṣu kaścidarthavyapāśrayaḥ ||18||

(18) For him there is no interest whatsoever in the performance of an action or its non-performance; nor does he depend on any creature for any object.

tasmādasaktaḥ satataṁ kāryaṁ karma samācara

asakto hyācarankarma paramāpnoti pūruṣaḥ ||19||

(19) Therefore, always perform your work, without attachment, which has to be done; for a man who works without attachment he attains the Supreme.

karmaṇaiva hi saṁsiddhimāsthitā janakādayaḥ

lokasaṁgrahamevāpi sampaśyankartumarhasi ||20||

(20) It is through action, that King Janaka and others attained perfection. Even with a view to the maintenance of the world-order, you must perform action.

yadyadācarati śreṣṭhastattadevetaro janaḥ

sa yatpramāṇaṁ kurute lokastadanuvartate ||21||

(21) Whatever a great man does, the others also do the same; whatever standard he sets, the people follow.

na me pārthāsti kartavyaṁ triṣu lokeṣu kiñcana

nānavāptamavāptavyaṁ varta eva ca karmaṇi ||22||

(22) There is nothing in all the three worlds, O'Arjuna, that has to be doṇe by Me, nor is there anything unattained that ought to be attained; yet, I engage Myself in action.

yadi hyahaṁ na varteyaṁ jātu karmaṇyatandritaḥ

mama vartmānuvartante manuṣyāḥ pārtha sarvaśaḥ ||23||

utsīdeyurime lokā na kuryāṁ karma cedaham

saṅkarasya ca kartā syāmupahanyāmimāḥ prajāḥ ||24||

(23, 24) For, should I not engage Myself in action unwearied, men would follow My path in all respects, O'Arjuna. These worlds would perish, if I did not perform action; and I would be the cause of confusion, disorder and the destruction of the people.

saktāḥ karmaṇyavidvānso yathā kurvanti bhārata
kuryādvidvāṅstathāsaktaścikīrṣurlokasaṅgraham ||25||

(25) As the ignorant man acts with attachment to action O'Arjuna, so should the wise man act without attachment, desiring the welfare of the world.

na buddhibhedaṁ janayedajñānāṁ karmasaṅginām
joṣayetsarvakarmāṇi vidvānyuktaḥ samācaran ||26||

(26) The wise man who is established in the Self should not unsettle the mind of the ignorant people who are attached to action; he should get them to perform all their duties, by performing action himself with devotion.

prakṛteḥ kriyamāṇāni guṇaiḥ karmāṇi sarvaśaḥ
ahaṅkāravimūḍhātmā kartāhamiti manyate ||27||

(27) All actions are performed—in all respects, by the modes of nature. The one whose mind is deluded by egoism, he thinks 'I am the doer'.

tattvavittu mahābāho guṇakarmavibhāgayoḥ
guṇā guṇeṣu vartanta iti matvā na sajjate ||28||

(28) But he, who knows the truth, about the respective spheres of modes (Gunas) and their functions O'Arjuna, he clearly understands that

the Gunas-as-senses move among the Gunas-as-objects; and he does not become attached.

prakṛterguṇasammūḍhāḥ sajjante guṇakarmasu
tānakṛtsnavido mandānkṛtsnavinna vicālayet ||29||

(29) Those who are deluded by the qualities (gunas) of nature they remain attached to the functions of the gunas. The man of wisdom should not unsettle the minds of the ignorant, who do not know the whole truth.

mayi sarvāṇi karmāṇi sannyasyādhyātmacetsā
nirāśīrnirmamo bhūtvā yudhyasva vigatajvaraḥ ||30||

(30) Therefore, dedicating all actions to Me, with your mind focused on the Self, being free from desire, egoism and mental stress, fight the battle.

ye me matamidaṁ nityamanutiṣṭhanti mānavāḥ
śraddhāvanto'nasūyanto mucyante te'pi karmabhiḥ ||31||

(31) Those men who constantly follow this teaching of Mine with faith and without cavilling, they are also liberated from the bondage of actions.

ye tvetadabhyasūyanto nānutiṣṭhanti me matam
sarvajñānavimūḍhāṅstānviddhi naṣṭānacetsaḥ ||32||

(32) But those who cavil at My teaching and do not follow it, know them to be absolutely ignorant, devoid of all knowledge and lost.

sadṛśaṁ ceṣṭate svasyāḥ prakṛterjñānavānapi

prakṛtiṁ yānti bhūtāni nigrahaḥ kiṁ kariṣyati ||33||

(33) Even the man of wisdom acts in accordance with his own nature; all beings follow their nature, what can restrain accomplish?

indriyasyendriyasyārthe rāgadveṣau vyavasthitau

tayorna vaśamāgacchettau hyasya paripanthinau ||34||

(34) Attachment and aversion for the objects of senses abide in the senses; one should not come under their sway, because they are his enemies.

śreyānsvadharmo viguṇaḥ paradharmātsvanuṣṭhitāt

svadharme nidhanaṁ śreyaḥ paradharmo bhayāvahaḥ ||35||

(35) Better is one's own duty, though devoid of merit, than the duty of another well performed. Even the death becomes blessed (gracious), in the performance of one's own duty; the duty of another is fraught with fear.

Arjuna Uvāca :

atha kena prayukto'yaṁ pāpaṁ carati pūruṣaḥ

anicchannapi vārṣṇeya balādiva niyojitaḥ ||36||

Arjuna said :

(36) But impelled by what, O'Kṛṣṇa, does a man commit sin, even against his will, as though driven by force?

Śrī Bhagavānuvāca :

kāma eṣa krodha eṣa rajoguṇasamudbhavaḥ

mahāśano mahāpāpmā vidhyenamiha vairiṇam ||37||

The Blessed Lord said :

(37) It is desire, it is anger born of the mode of passion; which is insatiable and most sinful. Know this to be the enemy in this respect.

dhūmenāvriyate vahniryathādarśo malena ca

yatholbenāvṛto garbhastathā tenedamāvṛtam ||38||

(38) As the flame is enveloped by the smoke, as a mirror by the dust and as an embryo by the amnion, so is this (knowledge) covered by that (desire).

āvṛtaṁ jñānametena jñānino nityavairiṇā

kāmarūpeṇa kaunteya duṣpūreṇānalena ca ||39||

(39) O' Arjuna, the wisdom stands enveloped by this constant enemy of the wise in the form of desire, which is insatiable like fire.

indriyāṇi mano buddhiraśyādhiṣṭhānamucyate

etairvimohayatyeṣa jñānamāvṛtya dehinam ||40||

(40) The senses, the mind and the intellect are said to be its seat; through these it deludes the embodied-self—by enveloping his wisdom.

tasmāttvamindriyāṇyādau niyamya bharatarṣabha

pāpmānaṁ prajahi hyenaṁ jñānavijñānanāśanam ||41||

(41) Therefore, O'Arjuna, control thy senses from the very beginning and kill this sinful destroyer of knowledge and experiential wisdom.

indriyāṇi parāṇyāhurindriyebhyaḥ paraṁ manaḥ
manasastu parā buddhiryo buddheḥ paratastu saḥ ||42||

(42) Senses are said to be superior (to the body), superior to senses is the mind; but higher than mind is the intellect and higher than the intellect is indeed the indwelling-Self.

evaṁ buddheḥ paraṁ buddhvā saṅstabhyātmānamātmanā
jahi śatruṁ mahābāho kāmarūpaṁ durāsadam ||43||

(43) Thus, knowing the indwelling-Self to be higher than the intellect and controlling the mind by the Self, O'Arjuna kill this enemy in the form of desire, which is very difficult to conquer.

'AUM TAT SAT'—Thus, in the Upanishad of the glorious Bhagawad Geeta, the science of the Brahman (Absolute) the scripture of yoga, the dialogue between Srī Kṛṣṇa and Arjuna—thus, ends the chapter three entitled "Karmayoga".

Chapter Four

JÑĀNA-KARMAYOGA

THE YOGA OF ACTION AND KNOWLEDGE

Śrī Bhagavānuvāca :

imaṁ vivasvate yogaṁ proktavānahamavyayam

vivasvānmanave prāha manurikṣvākave'bravīt ||1||

The Blessed Lord said :

(1) I taught this imperishable Yoga to Vivasvan (sun-god). Vivasvan taught it to Manu; and Manu taught to Ikshvaku.

evaṁ paramparāprāptamimaṁ rājarṣayo viduḥ

sa kāleneha mahatā yogo naṣṭaḥ parantapa ||2||

(2) Thus, handed down in regular succession, the royal sages knew this. But, through the long lapse of time, this yoga became lost to the world, O'Arjuna.

sa evāyaṁ mayā te'dya yogaḥ proktaḥ purātanaḥ

bhakto'si me sakhā ceti rahasyaṁ hyetaduttamam ||3||

(3) This same ancient Yoga has been declared to you by Me today; for you are My devotee and My friend. This is the Supreme secret.

Arjuna Uvāca :

aparaṁ bhavato janma paraṁ janma vivasvataḥ

kathametad vijānīyāṁ tvamādau proktavāniti ||4||

Arjuna said :

(4) Later on, was Thy birth and earlier to it was the birth of Vivasvan (sun-god). How can I understand this; that You ever taught this yoga in the beginning ?

Śrī Bhagavānuvāca :

bahūni me vyatītāni janmāni tava cā'rjuna

tānyahaṁ veda sarvāṇi na tvaṁ vettha parantapa ||5||

The Blessed Lord said :

(5) Many births of Mine have passed as well as of yours, O'Arjuna. I know them all, but you do not know them. O'scorcher of the foes.

ajo'pi sannavyayātmā bhūtānāmīśvaro'pi san

prakṛtiṁ svāmadhiṣṭhāya saṁbhavāmyātmamāyayā ||6||

(6) Though I am unborn, of imperishable nature and the Lord of all beings, yet, governing My own Nature, I come into being through My

power (Yoga Maya).

yadā yadā hi dharmasya glānirbhavati bhārata

abhyutthānamadharmasya tadātmānaṁ sṛjāmyaham ||7||

(7) Whenever there is decline of righteousness, (Dharma) and rise of unrighteousness, O'Arjuna, then I manifest Myself.

paritrāṇāya sādhūnāṁ vināśāya ca duṣkṛtām

dharmasaṅsthāpanārthāya saṁbhavāmi yuge yuge ||8||

(8) For the protection of the virtuous, for the destruction of the wicked, and for the establishment of righteousness (Dharma) I come into being from age to age.

janma karma ca me divyamevaṁ yo vetti tattvataḥ

tyaktvā dehaṁ punarjanma naiti māmeti so'rjuna ||9||

(9) He who, thus understands My divine birth and actions in essence; having abandoned the body, he is not born again. He comes to Me, O'Arjuna.

vītarāgabhayakrodhā manmayā māmupāśritāḥ

bahavo jñānatapasā pūtā madbhāvamāgatāḥ ||10||

(10) Liberated from desire, fear and anger with the mind absorbed in Me, taking refuge in Me, purified by the austerity of wisdom, many have

attained to My state of being.

ye yathā māṁ prapadyante tāṅstathaiva bhajāmyaham
mama vartmānuvartante manuṣyāḥ pārtha sarvaśaḥ ||11||

(11) In whatever way, men approach Me, so do I accept them; for all men follow My path in every way, O'Arjuna.

kāṅkṣantaḥ karmaṇāṁ siddhiṁ yajanta iha devatāḥ
kṣipraṁ hi mānuṣe loke siddhirbhavati karmajā ||12||

(12) Those who desire the fruits of their actions, worship the gods in this world, because the success is quickly attained by men, through action.

cāturvarṇyaṁ mayā sṛṣṭaṁ guṇakarmavibhāgaśaḥ
tasya kartāramapi māṁ viddhyakartāramavyayam ||13||

(13) The fourfold work order has been created by Me according to the differentiation of Guna and Karma. Though I am the creator, know Me as non-doer and immutable.

na māṁ karmāṇi limpanti na me karmaphale spṛhā
iti māṁ yo'bhijānāti karmabhirna sa badhyate ||14||

(14) Actions do not contaminate Me, because I have no desire for the fruit of actions. He who understands Me thus (in essence) is not bound by

actions.

evaṁ jñātvā kṛtaṁ karma pūrvairapi mumukṣubhiḥ

kuru karmaiva tasmāttvaṁ pūrvaiḥ pūrvataraṁ kṛtam ||15||

(15) Having known this, the seekers of liberation from ancient times have also performed their actions. Therefore, do thou also perform action as the ancients did in their times.

kiṁ karma kimakarmeti kavayo'pyatra mohitāḥ

tatte karma pravakṣyāmi yajjñātvā mokṣyase'śubhāt ||16||

(16) What is action? What is inaction?—Even men of wisdom are confused about it. Therefore, I must explain to you about action; by knowing which, you will be liberated from its evil effect.

karmaṇo hyapi boddhavyaṁ boddhavyaṁ ca vikarmaṇaḥ

akarmaṇaśca boddhavyaṁ gahanā karmaṇo gatiḥ ||17||

(17) One must understand the truth about action, and the truth about the prohibited action. Likewise, the truth about inaction should also be known; for, mysterious is the nature of action.

karmaṇyakarma yaḥ paśyedakarmaṇi ca karma yaḥ

sa buddhimānmanuṣyeṣu sa yuktaḥ kṛtsnakarmakṛt ||18||

(18) He, who sees inaction in action, and also action in inaction, he is wise among men. He is a

yogi, and a true performer of all actions.

yasya sarve samārambhāḥ kāmasaṅkalpavarjitāḥ
jñānāgnidagdhakarmāṇaṁ tamāhuḥ paṇḍitaṁ budhāḥ ||19||

(19) He whose undertakings are all free from self-centred personal desires, whose actions have been purified in the fire of wisdom—him, the wise call a sage.

tyaktvā karmaphalāsaṅgaṁ nityatṛpto nirāśrayaḥ
karmaṇyabhipravṛtto'pi naiva kiñcitkaroti saḥ ||20||

(20) Renouncing attachment to the fruits of action, ever contented and free from all kinds of dependence, he does not do anything, though fully engaged in action.

nirāśīryatacittātmā tyaktasarvaparigrahaḥ
śārīraṁ kevalaṁ karma kurvannāpnoti kilbiṣam ||21||

(21) Having no desires, with his mind and body fully controlled, who has given up the desire for all sorts of possessions and performs only the necessary actions for the body; he is not tainted by sin (he is not subject to evil).

yadṛcchālābhasantuṣṭo dvandvātīto vimatsaraḥ
samaḥ siddhāvasiddhau ca kṛtvāpi na nibadhyate ||22||

(22) Fully contented with whatever comes

along, who is free from the pairs of opposites and envy, balanced in success and failure, even though he acts, he is not bound.

gatasaṅgasya muktasya jñānāvasthitacetasaḥ

yajñāyācarataḥ karma samagraṁ pravilīyate ||23||

(23) He, who is totally unattached and liberated, whose mind is established in transcendental knowledge, who performs all his work in the spirit of yajña (selflessly)—his actions are entirely dissolved.

brahmārpaṇaṁ brahma havirbrahmāgnau brahmaṇā hutam

brahmaiva tena gantavyaṁ brahmakarmasamādhinā ||24||

(24) For him, the act of offering is Brahman (God), the melted butter and oblation is Brahman. The oblation is offered by Brahman into the fire, which is Brahman. Thus, Brahman alone is to be reached by him, who meditates on Brahman in his work.

daivamevāpare yajñaṁ yoginaḥ paryupāsate

brahmāgnāvapare yajñaṁ yajñenaivopajuhvati ||25||

(25) Some yogis perform sacrifice (yajña) to the gods alone; while others offer sacrifice (selfless action) by the sacrifice itself, into the fire of

Brahman.

śrotrādīnīndriyāṇyanye saṅyamāgniṣu juhvati

śabdādīnviṣayānanya indriyāgniṣu juhvati ||26||

(26) Some offer hearing and other senses as sacrifice into the fire of self-restraint; Others offer sound and the object of senses as sacrifice into the fire of the senses.

sarvāṇīndriyakarmāṇi prāṇakarmāṇi cāpare

ātmasaṁyamayogāgnau juhvati jñānadīpite ||27||

(27) Some others offer the functions of the senses and the activity of the vital force (prana) into the fire of the yoga of self-control, lighted by the flame of knowledge.

dravyayajñāstapoyajñā yogayajñāstathāpare

svādhyāyajñānayajñāśca yatayaḥ saṅśitavratāḥ ||28||

(28) Some others offer their material possessions (wealth), austerity and yoga as sacrifice; while others of self-restraint and rigid vows offer the scriptural studies and knowledge as sacrifice.

apāne juhvati prāṇaṁ prāṇe'pānaṁ tathāpare

prāṇāpānagatī ruddhvā prāṇāyāmaparāyaṇāḥ ||29||

(29) Yet others, who are devoted to the breath control, sacrifice the outgoing breath into

incoming and the incoming into outgoing, by restraining the movement of both.

apare niyatāhārāḥ prāṇānprāṇeṣu juhvati

sarve'pyete yajñavido yajñakṣapitakalmaṣāḥ ||30||

(30) Others, who regulate their diet, they pour as sacrifice their life-breath into the life-breath. All these are the knowers of sacrifice, whose sins have been destroyed by sacrifice.

yajñaśiṣṭāmṛtabhujo yānti brahma sanātanam

nā'yaṁ loko'styayajñasya kuto'nyaḥ kurusattama ||31||

(31) Those who eat the sacred remnants of the sacrifice, which is like nectar, they attain to the eternal Absolute. Even this world is not for him, who does not perform sacrifice (selfless action)—how then the other, O'Arjuna?

evaṁ bahuvidhā yajñā vitatā brahmaṇo mukhe

karmajānviddhi tānsarvānevaṁ jñātvā vimokṣyase ||32||

(32) Many forms of sacrifices are spread out before the Brahman (set forth as means of attaining Brahman in Vedas). Know them all as born of action; knowing thus, you will be liberated.

śreyāndravyamayādyajñājjñānayajñaḥ parantapa

sarvaṁ karmākhilaṁ pārtha jñāne parisamāpyate ||33||

(33) Superior is sacrifice of wisdom to the sacrifice of material objects, O'Arjuna. All actions in their entirety culminate in wisdom.

tadviddhi praṇipātena paripraśnena sevayā

upadekṣyanti te jñānaṁ jñāninastattvadarśinaḥ ||34||

(34) Attain this knowledge by prostration (humble reverence) by asking questions and by service. The men of wisdom, who have realized the truth will instruct you in knowledge.

yajjñātvā na punarmohamevaṁ yāsyasi pāṇḍava

yena bhūtānyaśeṣeṇa drakṣyasyātmanyatho mayi ||35||

(35) Knowing that, O'Arjuna, you will not again get deluded like this—by that knowledge you will see all beings without exception within yourself and then in Me.

api cedasi pāpebhyaḥ sarvebhyaḥ pāpakṛttamaḥ

sarvaṁ jñānaplavenaiva vṛjinaṁ santariṣyasi ||36||

(36) Even if you are the most sinful of all sinners, you will surely cross all the sins by the boat of knowledge alone.

yathaidhāṁsi samiddho'gnirbhasmasātkurute'rjuna

jñānāgniḥ sarvakarmāṇi bhasmasātkurute tathā ||37||

(37) Just as the blazing fire reduces the fuel

to ashes, O'Arjuna, similarly the fire of knowledge reduces all actions to ashes.

na hi jñānena sadṛśaṁ pavitramiha vidyate
tatsvayaṁ yogasaṅsiddhaḥ kālenātmani vindati ||38||

(38) Certainly, there is no purifier in this world like the 'transcendental knowledge'. He who becomes perfected in yoga, he experiences this, in his own-self, in due course of time.

śraddhāvānllabhate jñānaṁ tatparaḥ saṅyatendriyaḥ
jñānaṁ labdhvā parāṁ śāntimacireṇādhigacchati ||39||

(39) He, who is endowed with faith and who is devoted to it, who has disciplined his senses, he obtains knowledge. Having attained knowledge, he immediately attains Supreme-peace.

ajñaścāśraddadhānaśca saṅśayātmā vinaśyati
nāyaṁ loko'sti na paro na sukhaṁ saṁśayātmanaḥ ||40||

(40) The man who is ignorant, who has no faith, who is sceptical, he goes to destruction. For the suspicious man there is neither this world, nor the world beyond, nor any happiness.

yogasannyastakarmāṇaṁ jñānasañchinnasaṅśayam
ātmavantaṁ na karmāṇi nibadhnanti dhanañjaya ||41||

(41) He who has renounced actions by unity

in yoga, whose doubts have been destroyed by knowledge, and who is settled in the Self—actions do not bind him, O'Arjuna.

tasmādajñānasambhūtaṁ hṛtsthaṁ jñānāsinātmanaḥ
chittvainaṁ saṅśayaṁ yogamātiṣṭhottiṣṭha bhārata ||42||

(42) Therefore, with the sword of knowledge, cut asunder the doubt in your heart, which is born of ignorance. Take refuge in Yoga and stand up, O' Arjuna.

'AUM TAT SAT'—Thus, in the Upanishad of the glorious Bhagawad Geeta, the science of the Brahman (Absolute) the scripture of yoga, the dialogue between Srī Kṛṣṇa and Arjuna—thus, ends the chapter four entitled "Jñanakarmayoga".

Chapter Five

KARMA-SANNYĀSAYOGA

THE YOGA OF ACTION AND RENUNCIATION

Arjuna Uvāca :

sannyāsaṁ karmaṇāṁ kṛṣṇa punaryogaṁ ca śaṁsasi

yacchreya etayorekaṁ tanme brūhi suniścitam ||1||

Arjuna said :

(1) O' Kṛṣṇa, you praise the renunciation of actions and then again the practice of Yoga; (the performance of selfless action)—tell me for certain, which one of these two is decidedly better.

Śrī Bhagavānuvāca :

sannyāsaḥ karmayogaśca niḥśreyasakarāvubhau

tayos tu karmasannyāsāt karmayogo viśiṣyate ||2||

The Blessed Lord said :

(2) Renunciation and the yoga of action both lead to the highest Bliss; but of the two, yoga of action is superior to the renunciation of action.

jñeyaḥ sa nityasannyāsī yo na dveṣthi nā kāṅkṣati
nirdvandvo hi mahābāho sukham bandhātpramucyate ||3||

(3) He should be known as a perpetual renouncer, who neither hates nor desires and who is free from all dualities. O'Arjuna, he is indeed easily liberated from bondage.

sāṅkhyayogau pṛathag bālāḥ pravadaṇti na paṇditāḥ
ekamapyāsthitaḥ samyagubhayorvindate phalam ||4||

(4) Children, not the learned, speak of knowledge (Samkhya) and the Yoga of action as distinct. He who is truly established in either, attains the fruits of both.

yatsāṅkhyaiḥ prāpyate sthānaṁ tad yagairapi gamyate
ekaṁ sāṅkhyaṁ ca yogaṁ ca yaḥ paśyati sa paśyati ||5||

(5) The spiritual status which is obtained with the yoga of knowledge is also achieved with the yoga of action. He truly sees, who sees the knowledge and the yoga of action as one.

sannyāsastu māhabāho duḥkhamāptumayogataḥ
yogayukto munirbrahma nacireṇādhigacchati ||6||

(6) O'Arjuna, renunciation is indeed difficult to attain without yoga. The sage who is established in yoga, he definitely reaches the Brahman very quickly.

yogayukto viśuddhātmā vijitātmā jitendriyaḥ

sarvabhūtātmabhūtātmā kurvannapi na lipyate ||7||

(7) He, who is united with the Self in yoga, who is pure at heart, whose body and senses are under his control, who realizes his own Self, as the Self in all beings, he is not tainted by actions, while he performs.

naiva kiñcit karomīti yukto manyeta tattvavit

paśyaṇ śṛṇvan spṛśañ jighrann aśnan gacchan śvapan śvasan ||8||

pralapan visṛjan gṛhṇannunmiṣan nimiṣannapi

indriyāṇīndriyārtheṣu vartanta iti dhārayan ||9||

(8, 9) The knower of truth, who is united within, he believes 'I am not doing anything' even while—seeing, hearing, touching, smelling, eating, walking, sleeping, breathing, speaking, excreting, grasping, opening and closing the eyelids. He always remains convinced that the senses operate among the sense objects.

brahmaṇyādhāya karmāṇi saṅgaṁ tyaktvā karoti yaḥ

lipyate na sa pāpena padmapatramivāmbhasā ||10||

(10) He who performs all his actions, offering them to the Divine and abandons all attachment, he is not touched by sin, just as the lotus leaf is not tainted by water.

kāyena manasā buddhyā kevalairindriyairapi

yoginaḥ karma kurvanti saṅgaṁ tyaktvātmaśuddhaye ||11||

(11) The yogins perform their actions merely with the body, the mind, the intellect and the senses, without any attachment—for the purification of the self (heart).

yuktaḥ karmaphalaṁ tyaktvā śāntimāpnoti naiṣṭhikīm

ayuktaḥ kāmakāreṇa phale sakto nibadhyate ||12||

(12) He who is united within, having renounced the fruits of actions, attains the highest peace; but the disintegrated man being impelled by desire, remains attached to the fruits and becomes bound.

sarvakarmāṇi manasā sannyasyāste sukhaṁ vaśī

navadvāre pure dehī naiva kurvanna kārayan ||13||

(13) Mentally, renouncing the doership of all actions, the self-controlled embodied-self (Jivatma), rests peacefully in the city of nine gates, neither acting nor causing others to act.

na kartṛtvaṁ na karmāṇi lokasya sṛjati prabhuḥ

na karmaphalasaṁyogaṁ svabhāvastu pravartate ||14||

(14) The Lord does not create the agency nor the actions for the world; nor does he connect actions with their fruits. It is only the innate nature that operates.

nādatte kasyacit pāpaṁ na caiva sukṛtaṁ vibhuḥ

ajñānenāvṛtaṁ jñānaṁ tena muhyanti jantavaḥ ||15||

(15) The Omnipresent Lord takes neither the sin nor the virtue of any; the knowledge is enveloped by ignorance, therefore creatures are bewildered.

jñānena tu tadajñānaṁ yeṣāṁ nāśitamātmanaḥ

teṣāmādityavajjñānaṁ prakāśayati tat param ||16||

(16) To those, whose ignorance has been dispelled by the knowledge of the Self, for them, the knowledge reveals the Supreme Brahman like the Sun.

tadbuddhayastadātmānas tanniṣṭhās tatparāyaṇāḥ

gacchantyapunarāvṛttiṁ jñānanirdhūtakalmaṣāḥ ||17||

(17) Those, whose mind and intellect are totally merged in God, who remain established in unity, and consider that as their Supreme goal they reach the state from which there is no return—their sins being dispelled by knowledge.

vidyāvinayasaṁpanne brāhmaṇe gavi hastini

śuni caiva śvapāke ca paṇḍitāḥ samadarśinaḥ ||18||

(18) The man of wisdom looks with equanimity upon the Brahmin endowed with learning and humility, a cow, an elephant, and even a dog and a pariah.

ihaiva tairjitaḥ sargo yeṣāṁ sāmye sthitaṁ manaḥ
nirdoṣaṁ hi samaṁ brahma tasmād brahmaṇi te sthitāḥ ||19||

(19) Even here the world is conquered by those, whose mind is established in equality. Brahman is indeed flawless and the same everywhere, therefore, they are established in Brahman.

na prahṛṣyetpriyaṁ prāpya nodvijet prāpya cāpriyam
sthirabuddhirasaṁmūḍho brahmavid brahmaṇi sthitaḥ ||20||

(20) He who neither rejoices on receiving what is pleasant nor grieves on receiving the unpleasant; who is firm of understanding and undeluded; such a knower of Brahman is established in Brahman.

bāhyasparśeṣvasaktātmā vindatyātmani yat sukham
sa brahmayogayuktātmā sukham akṣayam aśnute ||21||

(21) When the embodied-self is not attached to the external objects of the senses, and finds happiness within the Self—he becomes united with Brahman in yoga and enjoys the eternal Bliss.

ye hi saṅsparaśajā bhoga duḥkhayonaya eva te
ādyantavantaḥ Kaunteya na teṣu ramate budhaḥ ||22||

(22) The enjoyments that are born of contacts with the sense objects are the source of pain; they have a beginning and an end, O'Arjuna. The wise man does not rejoice in them.

śaknotīhaiva yaḥ soḍhuṁ prākśarīravimokṣaṇāt

kāmakrodhodbhavaṁ vegaṁ sa yuktaḥ sa sukhī naraḥ ||23||

(23) He who in this world is able to resist the impulse, born out of desire and anger, before he gives up his body—he is indeed a yogi, he is a happy man.

yo'ntaḥsukho'ntarārāmas tathāntarjyotireva yaḥ

sa yogī brahmanirvāṇaṁ brahmabhūto'dhigacchati ||24||

(24) He who finds his happiness within, who rejoices within himself, who is illuminated from within—that yogi attains absolute liberation (Brahman Nirvana); because of his firm identification with Brahman.

labhante brahmanirvāṇam ṛṣayaḥ kṣīṇakalmaṣāḥ

chinnadvaidhā yatātmānaḥ sarvabhūtahite ratāḥ ||25||

(25) The Rishis obtain absolute freedom—whose sins have been destroyed and whose dualities are torn asunder. Who are self-controlled and always devoted to the welfare of all beings.

kāmakrodhaviyuktānaṁ yatīnāṁ yatacetasām

abhito brahmanirvāṇaṁ vartate viditātmanām ||26||

(26) The ascetics those are free from desire and anger, who have controlled their mind and have realized the Self; for them the eternal Bliss

(Brahmic Bliss) exists on all sides.

sparśān kṛtvā bahir bāhyāṅś cakṣuś caivāntare bhruvoḥ
prāṇāpānau samau kṛtvā nāsābhyantaracāriṇau ||27||
yatendriyamanobuddhir munirmokṣaparāyaṇaḥ
vigatecchābhayakrodho yaḥ sadā mukta eva saḥ ||28||

(27, 28) Shutting out the external sensory contacts, fixing the vision between the two eyebrows, controlling the outgoing and incoming breath flow, with the senses, mind and intellect fully restrained, and free from desire, fear and anger—the sage who aims at liberation, as his highest goal, he is verily liberated for ever.

bhoktākaraṁ yajñatapasāṁ sarvalokamaheśvaram
suhṛdaṁ sarvabhūtānāṁ jñātvā māṁ śāntimṛcchati ||29||

(29) Knowing Me as the enjoyer of all sacrifices and austerities, the great Lord of all the worlds and the well-wisher (friend) of all beings, one attains peace.

'AUM TAT SAT'—Thus, in the Upanishad of the glorious Bhagawad Geeta, the science of the Brahman (Absolute) the scripture of yoga, the dialogue between Srī Kṛṣṇa and Arjuna—thus, ends the chapter five entitled "Karma-sannyāsayoga".

Chapter Six

DHYĀNAYOGA

THE YOGA OF MEDITATION

Śrī Bhagavānuvāca :

anāśritaḥ karmaphalaṁ kāryaṁ karma karoti yaḥ

sa sannyāsī ca yogī ca na niragnir na cākriyaḥ ||1||

The Blessed Lord said :

(1) He who performs obligatory duties without depending upon the fruits of actions—he is a true renunciate (Sannyasi) and a yogi; not the one who has renounced the sacred fire and the performance of action.

yaṁ sannyāsamiti prāhur yogaṁ taṁ viddhi pāṇḍava

na hy asannyastasaṅkalpo yogī bhavati kaścana ||2||

(2) That which is called renunciation know that to be the yoga, O' Arjuna; for no one can become a yogi, without renouncing the selfish desires of the world.

āruruksor muner yogaṁ karma kāraṇamucyate

yogārūḍhasya tasyaiva śamaḥ kāraṇamucyate ||3||

(3) Action is considered to be the means for the sage who aspires to ascend in yoga; when he is established in yoga, tranquillity of mind is said to be the means.

yadā hi nendriyārtheṣu na karmasvanuṣajjate

sarvasaṅkalpasannyāsī yogārūḍhasta docyate ||4||

(4) When one becomes detached from the objects of senses and from actions, and has renounced all personal desires, then he is said to have ascended in Yoga.

uddharedātmanātmānaṁ nātmānamavasādayet

ātmai'va hyātmano bandhurātmaiva ripurātmanaḥ ||5||

(5) Let a man lift himself by his Self, Let him not degrade himself; for he himself is his own friend and he himself is his own enemy.

bandhurātmatmanastasya yenātmaivātmanā jitaḥ

anātmanastu śatrutve vartetātmaiva śatruvat ||6||

(6) To him who has conquered his lower-self by the Higher-Self, his Self becomes a friend; but for him who has not conquered his lower-self his own Self-acts as an enemy.

jitātmanaḥ praśāntasya paramātmā samāhitaḥ
śītoṣṇasukhaduḥkheṣu tathā mānāpamānayoḥ ||7||

(7) The self-controlled man, whose mind is perfectly serene and settled in the Supreme-Self, becomes balanced in cold and heat, in pleasure and pain, in honour and dishonour.

jñānavijñānatṛptātmā kūtastho vijitendriyaḥ
yukta ityucyate yogī samaloṣṭāśmakāñcanaḥ ||8||

(8) Who is satisfied with the knowledge and the experiential wisdom of the Self, who is steadfast and self-controlled, who considers a clod, a stone and a piece of gold alike; he is said to be established in yoga.

suhṛnmitrāryudāsīnamadhyasthadveṣyabandhuṣu
sādhuṣvapi ca pāpeṣu sambuddhirviśiṣyate ||9||

(9) He who regards the well-wishers, friends, enemies, indifferent, neutral, hateful, relatives, saint and the sinner alike, is indeed balanced and stands distinguished.

yogī yuñjīta satatamātmānaṁ rahasi sthitaḥ
ekākī yatacittātmā nirāśīraparigrahaḥ ||10||

(10) The yogi should constantly engage his mind in meditation, while living alone in solitude.

Having controlled his mind and body and being free from the sense of possession and desire.

śucau deśe pratiṣṭhāpya sthiramāsanamātmanaḥ
nātyucchritaṁ nātinīcaṁ cailājinakuśottaram ||11||

(11) On a clean spot, having established for himself a firm seat which is neither too high nor too low, and covered with a cloth, deer skin, and kusha-grass, one over the other.

tatraikāgraṁ manaḥ kṛtvā yatacittendriyakriyaḥ
upaviśyāsane yuñjyād yogamātmaviśuddhaye ||12||

(12) Sitting there, on his seat with one-pointed mind; controlling the functions of mind and senses; he should practise yoga for the purification of the self.

samaṁ kāyaśirogrīvaṁ dhārayannacalaṁ sthiraḥ
samprekṣya nāsikāgraṁ svaṁ diśaścānavalokayan ||13||

(13) Holding the trunk, head and neck straight, steady and still; he should fix the gaze on the tip of his nose, without looking in any other direction.

praśāntātmā vigatabhīrbrahmacārivrate sthitaḥ
manaḥ saṅyamya maccitto yukta āsīta matparaḥ ||14||

(14) Peaceful and fearless, steadfast in the vow

of celibacy, with mind fully disciplined and concentrated on Me; he should sit in yogic meditation—having Me as the Supreme goal.

yuñjannevaṁ sadā'tamānaṁ yogī niyatamānasaḥ
śāntiṁ nirvāṇaparamāṁ matsaṁsthāmadhigacchati ||15||

(15) Thus constantly uniting his mind with Me, the yogi of disciplined mind, attains peace; the Supreme Nirvana, which abides in Me.

nātyaśnatastu yogo'sti na caikāntamanaśnataḥ
na cāti svapnaśīlasya jāgrato naiva cārjuna ||16||

(16) Yoga is not for him who eats too much, nor for him who does not eat at all; it is not for him who sleeps too much, nor for him who is ever awake, O'Arjuna.

yuktāhāravihārasya yuktaceṣṭasya karmasu
yuktasvapnāvabodhasya yogo bhavati duḥkhahā ||17||

(17) The man who is regulated in diet and recreation, disciplined in the performance of work, who is regulated in sleep and wakefulness, for him the Yoga becomes the destroyer of pain.

yadā viniyataṁ cittām atmanyevāvatiṣṭhate
niḥspṛhaḥ sarvakāmebhyo yukta ityucyate tadā ||18||

(18) When the perfectly disciplined mind rests in the Self alone, and is free from the yearning for

the objects of desires, one is said to be united in Yoga.

yathā dīpo nivātastho neṅgate sopamā smṛtā

yogino yatacittasya yuñjato yogāmatmanaḥ ||19||

(19) As a lamp placed in a windless spot does not flicker, is the simile used for a yogi of subdued mind, who is practising to unite in Yoga with the Self.

yatroparamate cittaṁ niruddhaṁ yogasevayā

yatra caivātmanātmānaṁ paśyannātmani tuṣyati ||20||

(20) Where the mind becomes peaceful and restrained by the practice of Yoga, wherein one beholds the Self within the self, one rejoices in the Self alone.

sukhamātyantikaṁ yat tad buddhigrāhyamatīndriyam

vetti yatra na caivāyaṁ sthitaścalati tattvataḥ ||21||

(21) Where one experiences transcendental bliss, which is perceived only by the subtle intellect, and which is beyond the grasp of the senses, established in that state, one never moves from the essential truth.

yaṁ labdhvā cāparaṁ lābhaṁ manyate nādhikaṁ tataḥ

yasminsthito na duḥkhena guruṇāpi vicālyate ||22||

(22) Having obtained that which one considers nothing else superior to it; wherein established,

the individual is not shaken even by the deepest sorrow.

taṁ vidyād duḥkhasaṅyogaviyogaṁ yogasamjñitam

sa niścayena yoktavyo yogo'nirvinnacetasā ||23||

(23) This state is known by the name of Yoga which is free from the contacts of sorrow. This Yoga should be practised with determination and concentration of mind.

saṅkalpaprabhavān kāmāṅs tyaktvā sarvānaśeṣataḥ

manasaivendriyagrāmaṁ viniyamya samantataḥ ||24||

śanaiḥ śanairuparamed bhuddhayā dhṛtigṛhītayā

ātmasaṁsthaṁ manaḥ kṛtvā na kiñcidapi cintayet ||25||

(24, 25) Abandoning all desires which arise from the thoughts of the world and fully controlling the mind from the entire group of senses, let him gradually attain tranquillity, with the intellect held in firmness; having made the mind established in the Self, let him not think about anything else.

yato-yato niścarati manaścañcalam asthiram

tatas-tato niyamyaitad ātmanyeva vaśaṁ nayet ||26||

(26) For whatever reason, when the restless mind wanders away, he should restrain it and bring it under the control of Self alone.

praśāntamanasaṁ hyenaṁ yoginaṁ sukhamuttamam
upaiti śāntarajasaṁ brahmabhūtamakalmaṣam ||20||

(27) The Supreme Bliss comes to the yogi whose mind is at peace, whose passion (rajas) has been subdued, who is sinless and has become identified with the Brahman.

yuñjannevaṁ sadātmānaṁ yogī vigatakalmaṣaḥ
sukhena brahmasaṁsparśam atyantaṁ sukhamaśnute ||28||

(28) Thus constantly uniting the mind with the Self, the yogi becomes free from sins and easily attains the infinite Bliss of oneness with Brahman.

sarvabhūtasthamātmānaṁ sarvabhūtāni cātmani
īkṣate yogayuktātmā sarvatra samadarśanaḥ ||29||

(29) He whose self is established in Yoga, he beholds the self abiding in all beings and all beings in the Self. He sees equality everywhere.

yo māṁ paśyati sarvatra sarvaṁ ca mayi paśyati
tasyā'haṁ na praṇaśyāmi sa ca me na praṇaśyati ||30||

(30) He who sees Me everywhere and sees everything existing in Me, I am never out of sight for him, nor is he ever out of My sight.

sarvabhūtasthitaṁ yo māṁ bhajatyekatvamāsthitaḥ
sarvathā vartamānopi sa yogī mayi vartate ||31||

(31) He who, being established in oneness,

worships Me dwelling in all beings, that yogi ever resides in Me, though engaged in all forms of activities.

ātmaupamyena sarvatra samaṁ paśyati yo'rjuna
sukhaṁ vā yadi vā duḥkhaṁ sa yogī parmo mataḥ ||32||

(32) He who, through the reflections of his own-self, sees equality everywhere, be it pleasure or pain, he is considered a perfect yogi., O'Arjuna.

Arjuna Uvāca :

yo'yaṁ yogastvayā proktaḥ sāmyena madhūsudana
etasyāhaṁ na paśyāmi cañcalatvātsthitiṁ sthirām ||33||

Arjuna said :

(33) This Yoga of equanimity, which has been declared by you, O' Kṛṣṇa, I don't see that it can be steady and lasting because of the instability of the mind.

cañcalaṁ hi manaḥ kṛṣṇa pramāthi balavad dṛḍham
tasyāhaṁ nigrahaṁ manye vāyoriva suduṣkaram ||34||

(34) Mind is very restless O'Kṛṣṇa,—turbulent, powerful and very stubborn. I believe that it is as difficult to control as the wind.

Śrī Bhagavānuvāca :

asaṅśayaṁ mahābāho mano durnigrahaṁ calam
abhyāsena tu kaunteya vairāgyeṇa ca gṛhyate ||35||

The Blessed Lord said :

(35) Without doubt, O'mighty-armed (Arjuna), the mind is restless, very hard to control; but by practice and by dispassion O' son of Kunti, it can be controlled.

asaṅyatātmanā yogo duṣprāpa iti me matiḥ

vaśyātmanā tu yatatā śakyo'vāptumupāyataḥ ||36||

(36) The yoga is indeed very difficult to attain for a person of unrestrained mind—this is My opinion. But the self-controlled one, who strives ceaselessly, it becomes possible through proper practice.

Arjuna Uvāca :

ayatiḥ śraddhayopeto yogāccalitamānsaḥ

aprāpya yogasaṅsiddhiṁ kāṁ gatiṁ kṛṣṇa gacchati ||37||

Arjuna said :

(37) He who is endowed with full faith, but is undisciplined and whose mind slips away from yogic communion, having failed to attain perfection in yoga,—where does he go? O' Kṛṣṇa.

kaccinnobhayavibhraṣṭaś chinnābhramiva naśyati

apratiṣṭho māhābāho vimūḍho brahmaṇaḥ pathi ||38||

(38) Thus, fallen from both, doesn't he perish

like a dissipated cloud, O' Kṛṣṇa; lacking firm support and bewildered in the path that leads to the Brahman.

etanme saṅśayaṁ kṛṣṇa chetturmahasyaśeṣataḥ

tvadanyaḥ saṅśayasyāsya chettā na hyupapadyate ||39||

(39) This doubt of mine, O' Kṛṣṇa, Thou shouldst dispel completely; for no one else except You can clear this doubt.

Śrī Bhagavānuvāca :

pārtha nāiveha nāmutra vināśastasya vidyate

na hi kalyāṇakṛtkaścid durgatiṁ tāta gacchati ||40||

The Blessed Lord said :

(40) O'Arjuna, neither in this world nor hereafter there is any chance of destruction for him; for no one, who does the virtuous deeds ever comes to grief.

prāpya puṇyakṛtāṁ lokānuṣitvā śāśvatīḥ samaḥ

śucīnāṁ śrīmatāṁ gehe yogabhraṣṭo'bhijāyate ||41||

(41) Having attained to the world of the righteous, and having lived there for countless years; he who has fallen from yoga, is reborn in the family of the virtuous and prosperous.

athavā yogināmeva kule bhavati dhīmatām

etaddhi durlabhataraṁ loke janma yadīdṛśam ||42||

(42) Or he is born in a family of the enlightened yogins, although this type of birth is very difficult to obtain in this world.

tatra taṁ buddhisaṅyogaṁ labhate paurvadehikam
yatate ca tato bhūyaḥ saṅsiddhau kurunandana ||43||

(43) There, he regains with increased intuition, the knowledge of his previous birth and strives much more than before for perfection, O'Arjuna.

pūrvābhyāsena tenaiva hriyate hyavaśo'pi saḥ
jijñāsurapi yogasya śabdabrahmātivartate ||44||

(44) Initiated by the force of his former practice, he is carried on irresistibly. Even if he merely strives to know about yoga, he transcends the Sabad brahman.

prayatnādyatamānastu yogī saṅśuddhakilbiṣaḥ
anekajanmasaṅsiddhastato yāti parām gatim ||45||

(45) The yogi who strives earnestly, he becomes purified from all sins, perfected gradually through many births, he reaches the supreme state.

tapasvibhyo'dhiko yogī jñānibhyo'pi mato'dhikaḥ
karmibhyaścādhiko yogī tasmādyogī bhavā'rjuna ||46||

(46) The yogi is thought to be more revered than the ascetic, he is considered to be greater

than the man of knowledge; yogi is indeed superior to those who perform ritualistic actions. Therefore, Arjuna you be a yogi.

yogināmapi sarveṣāṁ madgatenāntarātmanā
śraddhāvānbhajate yo māṁ sa me yuktatamo mataḥ ||47||

(47) Among all the yogis, he who worships Me with full faith and devotion, with his mind focused on Me, I consider him to be the most devout yogi.

'AUM TAT SAT'—Thus, in the Upanishad of the glorious Bhagawad Geeta, the science of the Brahman (Absolute) the scripture of yoga, the dialogue between Srī Kṛṣṇa and Arjuna—thus, ends the chapter six entitled "Dhyānayoga".

Chapter Seven

JÑĀNAVIJÑĀNAYOGA

THE YOGA OF WISDOM AND KNOWLEDGE

Śrī Bhagavānuvāca :

mayyāsaktamanāḥ pārtha yogaṁ yuñjan madāsrayaḥ

asaṅśayaṁ samagraṁ māṁ yathā jñasyasi tacchṛṇu ||1||

The Blessed Lord Said :

(1) With your mind focused on Me, O' Arjuna, and taking refuge in Me through the practice of yoga—listen, how you can know Me, for sure in My entirety.

jñānaṁ te'haṁ savijñānamidaṁ vakṣyāmyaśeṣataḥ

yajjñātvā ne'ha bhūyo'nyajjñātavyam avaśiṣyate ||2||

(2) I shall teach you in detail the wisdom along with the experiential knowledge which makes it distinguished; having known which nothing else remains to be known.

manuṣyānāṁ sahasreṣu kaścid yatati siddhaye

yatatāmapi siddhānāṁ kaścinmāṁ vetti tattvataḥ ||3||

(3) Among thousands of men, scarcely one strives for perfection; and those who strive and attain perfection, scarcely there is one, who knows Me in essence.

bhūmirāpo'nalo vāyuḥ khaṁ mano buddhireva ca
ahaṅkāra itīyaṁ me bhinnā prakṛtiraṣṭadhā ||4||
apareyam itastvanyāṁ prakṛtiṁ viddhi me parām
jīvabhūtāṁ mahābāho yayedaṁ dhāryate jagat ||5||

(4, 5) Earth, Water, Fire, Air, Ether, Mind, Intellect and Ego, this is the division of My eight-fold Prakrti (Nature). This is My lower Nature, and other than this is My transcendental Nature. It is the life-element, O'Arjuna, by which this universe is sustained.

etad yonīni bhūtāni sarvāṇītyupadhāraya
ahaṁ kṛtsnasya jagataḥ prabhavaḥ pralayastathā ||6||

(6) Know, that all the created beings have evolved from this twofold nature. I am the origin of the whole universe, as well as the dissolution.

mattaḥ parataraṁ nānyat kiñcid asti dhanañjaya
mayi sarvamidaṁ protaṁ sūtre maṇigaṇā iva ||7||

(7) There is nothing else besides Me, O'Arjuna. Everything is strung on Me, like the clusters of gems on a string.

raso'hamapsu kaunteya prabhā'smi śaśisūryayoḥ

praṇavaḥ sarvavedeṣu śabdaḥ khe pauruṣaṁ nṛṣu ||8||

(8) I am the taste in water, O'Arjuna. I am the radiance in the moon and in the sun. I am the sacred syllable 'AUM' in all the Vedas; sound in the ether and virility in men.

puṇyo gandhaḥ pṛthivyāṁ ca tejaścāsmi vibhāvasau

jīvanaṁ sarvabhūteṣu tapasca'śmi tapasviṣu ||9||

(9) I am the pure fragrance in the earth and the brilliance in the fire. I am the life in all beings, and austerity in ascetics.

bījaṁ māṁ sarvabhūtānāṁ viddhi pārtha sanātanam

buddhir buddhimatāmasmi tejas tejasvināmaham ||10||

(10) Know Me, to be the eternal seed of all beings, O'Arjuna. I am the intelligence of the intelligent and the brilliance of the brilliant.

balaṁ balavatāṁ cāhaṁ kāmarāgavivarjitam

dharmāviruddho bhūteṣu kāmo'smi bhartarṣabha ||11||

(11) Of the strong, I am the strength, which is devoid of passion and attachment; in all beings I am that desire, which is not opposed by Dharma (righteousness) O'Arjuna.

ye cai'va sātvikā bhāvā rājasāstāmasāśca ye

matta eve'ti tān viddhi na tvahaṁ teṣu te mayi ||12||

(12) Know that all those states of *sattva, rajas* and *tamas* originate from Me alone. I am not in them yet, they are in Me.

tribhir guṇamayair bhāvairebhiḥ sarvamidaṁ jagat
mohitaṁ nābhijānāti māmebhyaḥ paramavyayam ||13||

(13) The whole world is deluded by these three qualities originating from the Prakirti (Nature), and fails to recognize Me; who is beyond them and imperishable.

daivī hyeṣā guṇamayī mama māyā duratyayā
māmeva ye prapadyante māyām etāṁ taranti te ||14||

(14) The Divine illusion (Maya) of Mine consisting of three qualities *(gunas)* of nature is very difficult to transcend. However, those who take refuge in Me alone, cross over this illusion (Maya).

na māṁ duṣkṛtino mūḍhāḥ prapadyante narādhamāḥ
māyayāphṛtajñānā āsuraṁ bhāvamāsritāḥ ||15||

(15) The evil-doers, deluded and the lowest among men do not seek refuge in Me; being deluded by the illusive nature (Maya), they lack proper knowledge and follow the ways of the demons.

caturvidhā bhajante māṁ janāḥ sukṛtino'rjuna
ārto jijñāsurarthārthī jñānī ca bharatarṣabha ||16||

(16) Four kinds of virtuous men worship Me, O'Arjuna. These are the distressed, the seeker of knowledge, the seeker of wealth, and the man of wisdom O'Bharata.

teṣāṁ jñānī nityayukta ekabhaktir viśiṣyate
priyo hi jñānino'tyarthamahaṁ sa ca mama priyaḥ ||17||

(17) Of these, the man of wisdom, who is ever united with Me in yoga, through single minded-devotion, is the foremost. I am extremely dear to the man of wisdom and he too is very dear to Me.

udārāḥ sarva evaite jñānī tvātmaiva me matam
āsthitaḥ sa hi yuktātmā māmevānuttamāṁ gatim ||18||

(18) All these are noble indeed, but the man of wisdom I regard to be My very Self; for he is steadfast, ever united in the Self, and has resorted to Me alone as the Supreme goal.

bahūnāṁ janmanām ante jñānavān māṁ prapadyate
vāsudevaḥ sarvamiti sa mahātmā sudurlabhaḥ ||19||

(19) At the end of many births, the man of wisdom seeks refuge in Me alone, realizing that 'Vasudeva is all.' It is indeed very difficult to find such a great soul (Mahatma).

kāmais tais-tair hṛtajñānāḥ prapadyante'nyadevatāḥ
taṁ-taṁ niyamamāsthāya prakṛtyā niyatāḥ svayā ||20||

(20) Those whose wisdom has been distorted by desires, resort to other gods, observing this or that rite; swayed by their own inherent nature.

yo-yo yāṁ-yāṁ tanuṁ bhaktaḥ śraddhayārcitumicchati
tasya-tasyācalāṁ śraddhāṁ tāmeva vidadhāmyaham ||21||

(21) Whatever form a devotee seeks to worship with faith—I make his faith in that firm and unflinching.

sa tayā śraddhayā yuktas tasyā'rādhanamīhate
labhate ca tataḥ kāmān mayaiva vihitānhi tān ||22||

(22) Endowed with steadfast faith, he engages in the worship of that form and obtains the objects of his desire, verily granted in reality by Me alone.

antavattu phalaṁ teṣāṁ tad bhavaty alpamedhasām
devān devāyajo yānti madbhaktā yānti māmapi ||23||

(23) The rewards attained by these people of limited understanding are temporary. The worshippers of gods go to gods, but My devotees come to Me.

avyaktaṁ vyaktimāpannaṁ manyante māmabuddhayaḥ
param bhavamajānanto mamāvyayamanuttamam ||24||

(24) The ignorant regard Me, the unmanifest,

as having manifestation, they do not know My Supreme Nature, which is unchanging and unsurpassed.

nāhaṁ prakāśaḥ sarvasya yogamāyāsamāvṛtaḥ
mūḍho'yaṁ nābhijānāti loko mām ajamavyayam ||25||

(25) I am not revealed to all, veiled by My Yoga-Maya (divine potency). The deluded ones in this world, do not recognize Me as the unborn and the imperishable Supreme spirit.

vedāhaṁ samatītāni vartamānāni cā'rjuna
bhaviṣyāṇi ca bhūtāni māṁ tu veda na kaścana ||26||

(26) I know all the beings of the past, the present, O'Arjuna and even the future, but no one knows Me.

icchādveṣasamutthena dvandvamohena bhārata
sarvabhūtāni saṁmohaṁ sarge yānti parantapa ||27||

(27) Through the delusion of the pairs of opposites, arising from desire and aversion, O'Arjuna, all the creatures become subject to delusion at birth, O'Parantapa.

yeṣāṁ tvantagataṁ pāpaṁ jnānāṁ puṇyakarmaṇām
te dvandvamohanirmuktā bhajante māṁ dṛḍhavratāḥ ||28||

(28) But the men of virtuous deeds, whose

sins have come to an end, those are liberated from the delusion of the pairs of opposites, they worship Me, with firm resolve.

jarāmaraṇamokṣāya māmāśritya yatanti ye
te brahma tadviduḥ kṛtsnamadhyātmaṁ karma cākhilam ||29||

(29) Those who take refuge in Me and strive for deliverance from old age and death, they know all about the absolute Brahman, the Self and the entire field of actions.

sādhibhūtādhidaivaṁ māṁ sadhiyajnaṁ ca ye viduḥ
prayāṇakāle'pi ca māṁ te vidur yuktacetasaḥ ||30||

(30) Those who realize Me within the Adhibuta, in the Adhidaiva and in the Adhiyajña, also realize Me at the time of death with their minds united in Yoga.

'AUM TAT SAT'—Thus, in the Upanishad of the glorious Bhagawad Geeta, the science of the Brahman (Absolute) the scripture of yoga, the dialogue between Srī Kṛṣṇa and Arjuna—thus, ends the chapter seven entitled "Jñanavijñanayoga".

Chapter Eight

AKṢARABRAHMAYOGA

THE YOGA OF THE IMPERISHABLE BRAHMAN

Arjuna Uvāca :

kiṁ tad brahma kim adhyātmaṁ kiṁ karma puroṣottama
adhibhūtaṁ ca kiṁ proktam adhidaivaṁ kim ucyate ||1||

Arjuna Said :

(1) What is Brahman? What is *adhyatma*? What is action? O'Supreme person. What is called *adhibuta*? And what is said to be *adhidaiva*?

adhiyajñaḥ kathaṁ ko'tra dehe'smin madhusūdana
prayāṇakāle ca kathaṁ jñeyo'si niyatātmabhiḥ ||2||

(2) Who and how is Adhiyajña here in this body, O'Kṛṣṇa? And how You are to be realized at the time of death by the self-controlled?

Śrī Bhagavānuvāca :

akṣaraṁ brahma paramaṁ svabhāvo'dhyātmamucyate
bhūtabhāvodbhavakaro visargaḥ karmasaṁjñitaḥ ||3||

The Blessed Lord said :

(3) The Supreme imperishable is Brahman; Its essential nature is known as *adhyatma.* The creative force which brings forth the existence of beings is called Karma (action).

adhibhūtaṁ kṣaro bhāvaḥ puruṣaś cādhidaivatam
adhiyajño'ham evātra dehe dehabhṛtāṁ vara ||4||

(4) *Adhibuta* pertains to My perishable nature; and the conscious principle Purusha is the *adhidaiva.* I am the *adhiyajña* here in this body, O' Arjuna.

antakāle ca māmeva smaran muktvā kalevaram
yaḥ prayāti sa madbhāvaṁ yāti nāstyatra saṅśayaḥ ||5||

(5) At the time of death, he who departs from the body thinking of Me alone, he attains to My essential nature, there is no doubt of this.

yaṁ-yaṁ vāpi smaran bhāvaṁ tyajatyante kalevaram
taṁ-tamevaiti kaunteya sadā tadbhāvabhāvitaḥ ||6||

(6) Whatever a person thinks at the time of his death while leaving his body, to that only he goes, O' Kaunteya, because of his being constantly absorbed in that thought.

tasmāt sarveṣu kāleṣu māmanusmara yudhya ca
mayyarpitamanobuddhir māmevaiṣyasyasaṅśayam ||7||

(7) Therefore at all times, think of Me alone and fight the battle. With your mind and intellect thus fixed on Me, Thou shall surely come to Me alone.

abhyāsayogayuktena cetasā nānyagāminā
paramaṁ puruṣaṁ divyaṁ yāti pārthānucintayan ||8||

(8) He who is established in the yogic meditation through constant practice, and does not let his mind wander after anything else, he surely attains the Supreme resplendent Divine Purusha, O'Arjuna.

kaviṁ purāṇamanuśāsitāra-
maṇoraṇīyānsamanusmared yaḥ
sarvasya dhātāramacintyarūpa
mādityavarṇaṁ tamasaḥ parastāt ||9||

(9) He, who contemplates on the Omniscient, the Primordial, the Ruler, subtler than an atom, the sustainer of all, the inconceivable, effulgent like the sun and beyond the darkness of ignorance.

prayāṇkāle manasā'calena
bhaktyā yukto yogabalena caiva
bhruvormadhye prāṇamāveśya samyak
sa taṁ paraṁ puruṣamupaiti divyam ||10||

(10) At the time of death with a steadfast mind, endowed with devotion and the power of Yoga,

who can firmly hold the life-breath in the middle of the two eyebrows, he surely reaches that resplendent supreme purusha.

yad akṣaraṁ vedavido vadanti
viśanti yad yatayo vītarāgaḥ
yad icchanto brahmacaryaṁ caranti
tatte padaṁ saṅgraheṇa pravakṣye ||11||

(11) That state which the knowers of Vedas call eternal, where in the ascetics enter, being free from attachment and desiring which they practise continence—that goal I must declare to you briefly.

sarvadvārāṇi saṅyamya mano hṛdi nirudhya ca
mūrdhanyādhāyātmanaḥ prāṇamāsthito yogadhāraṇām ||12||
omityekākṣaraṁ brahma vyāharan mām anusmaran
yaḥ prayāti tyajan dehaṁ sa yāti paramāṁ gatim ||13||

(12, 13) Having closed all the doors of senses and firmly restoring the mind in the heart and the life-breath in the crown of the head; established in the yogic concentration he who utters the single syllable AUM the Supreme Brahman and remembers Me while departing from his body, he certainly attains the Supreme Goal.

ananyacetāḥ satataṁ yo māṁ smarati nityaśaḥ
tasyā'haṁ sulabhaḥ pārtha nityayuktasya yoginaḥ ||14||

(14) He who constantly remembers Me with undivided attention, to him I am easily attainable, O'Partha, since he is ever united in Yoga.

mām upetya punarjanma duḥkhālayamaśāśvatam

nāpnuvanti mahātmānaḥ saṁsiddhiṁ paramāṁ gatāḥ ||15||

(15) Having come to Me, these great souls are not born again (here) which is the abode of sorrow and is transitory, for they have reached the highest perfection.

ābrahmabhuvanāllokāḥ punarāvartino'rjuna

māmupetya tu kaunteya punarjanma na vidyate ||16||

(16) From the realm of the Supreme creator, all the worlds are subject to return again and again, O' Arjuna. But having attained Me, O' son of Kunti, there is no rebirth.

sahasrayugaparyantamaharyad brahmaṇo viduḥ

rātriṁ yugasahasrāntāṁ te'horātravido janāḥ ||17||

(17) Those who know that the day of Brahma extends to a thousand epochs (yugas) and also the night extends to a thousand epochs, they are the knowers of the day and night (reality about time).

avyaktād vyaktayaḥ sarvāḥ prabhavanty aharāgame

rātryāgame pralīyante tatraivāvyaktasañjñake ||18||

(18) From the unmanifested, all the manifestations emerge at the commencement of the Brahma's day; at the coming of the night, they merge verily into that alone, which is called unmanifested.

bhūtagrāmaḥ sa evāyaṁ bhūtvā-bhūtvā pralīyate
rātryāgame'vaśaḥ pārtha prabhavatyaharāgame ||19||

(19) The multitude of beings, being born again and again, are dissolved helplessly at the coming of the night, O' Partha. It comes forth again at the beginning of the day.

parastasmāttu bhāvo'nyo'vyakto'vyaktāt sanātanaḥ
yaḥ sa sarveṣu bhūteṣunaśyatsu na vinaśyati ||20||

(20) Beyond this unmanifested, verily there is another unmanifested, Eternal, which does not perish even when all existence perish.

avyakto'kṣara ityuktastamāhuḥ paramāṁ gatim
yaṁ prāpya na nivartante taddhāma paramaṁ mama ||21||

(21) This Unmanifested and Imperishable is said to be the highest goal, upon attaining which, there is no return. That is My Supreme Abode.

puruṣaḥ sa paraḥ pārtha bhaktyā labhyastvananyayā
yasyāntaḥsthāni bhūtāni yena sarvamidaṁ tatam ||22||

(22) That Supreme transcendent Purusha, O'Arjuna, is attainable by undivided devotion; within whom all the beings reside and by whom all this is pervaded.

yatra kāle tvanāvṛttimāvṛttiṁ caiva yoginaḥ

prayātā yānti taṁ kālaṁ vakṣyāmi bharatarṣabha ||23||

(23) The time in which the yogis do not return after they depart and also the time when they do return again, of that, I shall tell you, O' best of the Bharatas (Arjuna).

agnir jyotirahaḥ śuklaḥ ṣaṇmāsā uttrāyaṇam

tatra prayātā gacchanti brahma brahmavido janāḥ ||24||

(24) Fire, light, the day time, the moonlit fortnight, the six months of the sun's northern course—departing in that time; the men who know Brahman go to Brahman.

dhūmo rātristathā kṛṣṇaḥ ṣaṇmāsā dakṣiṇāyanam

tatra cāndramasaṁ jyotiryogī prāpya nivartate ||25||

(25) Smoke, the night time, the dark lunar fortnight, the six months of the sun's southern course—having obtained the lunar light, the yogi returns (to the world of mortals).

śuklakṛṣṇe gatī hyete jagataḥ śāśvate mate

ekayā yāty anāvṛtti manyayā'vartate punaḥ ||26||

(26) The bright and the dark paths of the world are verily thought to be perennial. By the one a person leaves not to return, while by the other he returns again.

naite sṛtī pārtha jānan yogī muhyati kaścana
tasmāt sarveṣu kāleṣu yogayukto bhavārjuna ||27||

(27) Knowing these two paths, O'Arjuna, the yogi is not deluded. Therefore, at all times, stay united in Yoga, O'Arjuna.

vedeṣu yajñeṣu tapaḥsu caiva
dāneṣu yat puṇyaphalaṁ pradiṣṭam
atyeti tat sarvamidaṁ viditvā
yogī paraṁ sthānamupaiti cādyam ||28||

(28) The yogi, who realizes this profound truth, he transcends all the rewards of the meritorious deeds attached to the study of the Vedas, performance of sacrifices, austerities, and charities—he attains the Supreme primal status.

'AUM TAT SAT'—Thus, in the Upanishad of the glorious Bhagawad Geeta, the science of the Brahman (Absolute) the scripture of yoga, the dialogue between Srī Kṛṣṇa and Arjuna—thus, ends the chapter eight entitled "Aksarabrahmayoga".

Chapter Nine

RAJAVIDYA RAJAGUHYAYOGA

THE YOGA OF THE SOVEREIGN SCIENCE AND SOVEREIGN SECRET

Śrī Bhagavānuvāca :

idaṁ tu te guhyatamaṁ pravakṣyāmy anasūyave

jñānaṁ vijñānasahitaṁ yajjñātvā mokṣyase'śubhāt ||1||

The Blessed Lord said :

(1) To thee, who does not cavil, I shall now unfold the most profound secret of wisdom combined with the experiential knowledge, by knowing which you will be released from evil.

rājavidyā rājaguhyaṁ pavitramidamuttamam

pratyakṣāvagamaṁ dharmyaṁ susukhaṁ kartumavyayam ||2||

(2) This is the sovereign wisdom, the sovereign mystery, the most purifying excellent and easy to comprehend by direct experience. It is in accordance with the Dharma (righteousness) and

renders happiness. It is easy to accomplish and imperishable.

aśraddadhānāḥ puruṣā dharmasyā'sya parantapa
aprāpya māṁ nivartante mṛtyusaṁsārvartmani ||3||

(3) Persons lacking faith and reverence in the sacred doctrine (Dharma) O' Arjuna, fail to attain Me. They revolve in the path of the world of death.

mayā tatamidaṁ sarvaṁ jagadavyaktamūrtinā
matsthāni sarvabhūtāni na cāhaṁ teṣvavasthitaḥ ||4||

(4) This whole universe is pervaded by Me, in My unmanifest aspect. All the beings exist in Me, but I do not dwell in them.

na ca matsthāni bhūtāni paśya me yogamaiśvaram
bhutabhṛanna ca bhūtastho mamātmā bhūtabhāvanaḥ ||5||

(5) Nor do the beings exist in Me; behold My divine Yoga! I Myself am the creator and sustainer of all beings, yet I do not dwell in them.

yathākāśasthito nityam vāyuḥ sarvatrago mahān
tathā sarvāni bhūtāni matsthānītyupadhāraya ||6||

(6) As the mighty wind, always rests in the ether, while it moves everywhere; likewise know thou, that all created beings rest in Me.

sarvabhūtāni kaunteya prakṛtiṁ yānti māmikām
kalpakṣaye punastāni kalpādau visṛjāmyaham ||7||

(7) All beings, O' Kaunteya (Arjuna), go into My Nature, at the end of each *kalpa* and again at the beginning of the next *kalpa,* I send them forth again.

prakṛtiṁ svamavaṣṭabhya visṛjāmi punaḥ-punaḥ
bhūtagrāmamimaṁ kṛtsnam avaśaṁ prakṛter vaśāt ||8||

(8) Having hold on My nature, I send forth again and again the multitude of beings, subject to the helplessness of their own nature.

na ca māṁ tāni karmāṇi nibadhnanti dhanañjaya
udāsīnavadāsīnamasaktaṁ teṣu karmasu ||9||

(9) These actions do not bind Me, O' Dhananjaya (Arjuna), for I remain seated like the one unconcerned and unattached in those actions.

mayādhyakṣeṇa prakṛtiḥ sūyate sacarācaram
hetunānena kaunteya jagad viparivartate ||10||

(10) Under My supervision, Nature gives birth to all, the moving and the unmoving—by this means O' Kaunteya (Arjuna) the world revolves.

avajānanti māṁ mūḍhā mānuṣīṁ tanumāśritam
paraṁ bhāvamajānanto mama bhūtamaheśvaram ||11||
moghāśā moghakarmāṇo moghajñānā vicetasaḥ
rākṣasīmāsurīṁ caiva prakṛtiṁ mohinīṁ śritāḥ ||12||

(11, 12) The fools disregard Me, dwelling in human form. They do not know My transcendental nature, as the great Lord of all beings. With vain hopes, vain actions, and with vain knowledge they senselessly become possessed of the deceitful nature of demons and monsters.

mahātmānastu māṁ pārtha daivīṁ prakṛtim āśritāḥ

bhajantyananyamanaso jñātvā bhūtādimavyayam ||13||

(13) But the great souls, O'Partha (Arjuna), resorting to the divine nature, devote themselves to Me, with undistracted mind; knowing Me as the source of entire creation and imperishable.

satataṁ kīrtayanto māṁ yatantaś ca dṛḍhavratāḥ

namasyantaś ca māṁ bhaktyā nityayuktā upāsate ||14||

(14) Always singing My glories and endeavouring with determined vows, prostrating before Me with love and humility, they worship Me with steadfast devotion.

jñānayajñena cāpyanye yajanto māmupāsate

ekatvena pṛthaktvena bahudhā viśvatomukham ||15||

(15) Others worship Me through their offerings of integral knowledge, as the One, as distinct and as manifold; facing in all directions.

ahaṁ kraturahaṁ yajñaḥ svadhāhamahamauṣadham
mantro'ham ahamevājyam ahamagnirahaṁ hutam ||16||

(16) I am the Vaidika ritual and also the yajña, I am the offering given to ancestors, I am the medicinal herb of oblation. I am the sacred hymn, I am the clarified butter, I am the fire, I am the act of offering the oblation.

pitāhamasya jagato mātā dhātā pitāmahaḥ
vedyaṁ pavitramoṅkāra ṛksāma yajureva ca ||17||
gatir bhartā prabhuḥ sākṣī nivāsaḥ śaraṇaṁ suhṛt
prabhavaḥ pralayaḥ sthānaṁ nidhānaṁ bījamavyayam ||18||

(17, 18) I am the Father of this world and also the Mother, the sustainer and the Grandfather. I am the object of sacred knowledge, I am the purifier and the sacred syllable 'Aum.' I am *Rigveda, Samveda* and also the *Yajurveda.* I am the goal, the supporter, the Lord, the witness, the abode, the refuge, and the well-wisher. I am the origin and the dissolution, the resting place, the store-house and the imperishable seed of the universe.

tapāmyahamahaṁ varṣaṁ nigṛhṇāmyutsṛjāmi ca
amṛtaṁ caiva mṛtyuś ca sadasaccāhmarjuna ||19||

(19) I radiate heat, I withhold and send forth

the rain, I am immortality as well as death, I am being as well as non-being, O'Arjuna (existence and non-existence).

traividyā māṁ somapāḥ pūtapāpā
yajñairiṣṭvā svargatiṁ prārthayante
te puṇyāmāsādya surendrālokam
aśnanti divyān divi devabhogān ||20||

(20) The knowers of the three *Vedas,* who partake *soma* and are purified of all sins, who perform yajña seeking to reach the heaven; they surely obtain the holy world of the Lord of gods, and enjoy the celestial pleasures of the gods.

te taṁ bhuktvā svargalokaṁ viśālaṁ
kṣīṇe puṇye martyalokaṁ viśanti
evaṁ trayīdharmamanuprapannā
gatāgatṁ kāmakāmā labhante ||21||

(21) Having enjoyed the extensive heavenly world, they enter again into the world of mortals upon the exhaustion of their virtuous deeds. Thus confirming to the doctrine enjoined in the three *Vedas* and desirous of worldly enjoyments, they repeatedly come and go.

ananyāścintayanto māṁ ye janaḥ paryupāsate
teṣāṁ nityābhiyuktānāṁ yogaksemaṁ vahāmyaham ||22||

(22) The men who worship Me alone with undivided devotion, to those ever united in thought with Me, I bring full security and personally attend to their needs.

ye'pyanyadevatābhaktā yajante śraddhāyanvitāḥ
te'pi māmeva kaunteya yajantyavidhipūrvakam ||23||

(23) Even those who are the devotees of other gods and worship them with faithful reverence, even they O' Kaunteya, worship Me alone in essence, though not in accordance with the right approach.

ahaṁ hi sarvayajñānāṁ bhoktā ca prabhureva ca
na tu mām abhijānanti tattvenātaścyavanti te ||24||

(24) I alone am the receiver of all offerings and I alone am the Lord; but they do not know Me in essence, hence they fall.

yānti devavratā devān pitṝn yānti pitṛvratāḥ
bhūtāni yānti bhūtejyā yānti madyājino'pi mām ||25||

(25) The worshippers of gods go to the gods, the worshippers of manes reach the manes and of the evil spirits (Bhuta) go to the evil spirits. Those who worship Me alone, they surely come to Me.

patraṁ puṣpaṁ phalaṁ toyaṁ yo me bhaktyā prayacchati
tadahaṁ bhaktyupahṛtamaśnāmi prayatātmanaḥ ||26||

(26) A leaf, flower, fruit, water; whoever offers Me with loving devotion, I accept the pious offering of the pure minded with great joy.

yatkaroṣi yad aśnāsi yajjuhoṣi dadāsi yat

yat tapasyasi kaunteya tat kuruṣva madarpaṇam ||27||

(27) Whatever you do, whatever you eat, whatever you offer in sacrifice (yajña), whatever you give as charity, whatever austerity you practice O' Kaunteya—perform that as an offering to Me.

śubhāśubhaphalairevaṁ mokṣyase karmabandhanaiḥ

sannyāsayogayuktātmā vimukto māmupaiṣyasi ||28||

(28) Thus, you will remain free from the bonds of actions, yielding auspicious and inauspicious results. With the mind ever united in the Self with the Yoga of renunciation, you will be liberated and come to Me.

samo'haṁ sarvabhūteṣu na me dveṣyo'sti na priyaḥ

ye bhajanti tu māṁ bhaktyā mayi te teṣu cāpyaham ||29||

(29) I am alike to all beings; to Me there is none hateful or dear, but those who worship Me with devotion are in Me and I am also in them.

api cetsu durācāro bhajate mām ananyabhāk

sādhureva sa mantavyaḥ samyag vyavasito hi saḥ ||30||

(30) Even if the most wicked person worships Me with undivided devotion, he too should be regarded a saint, for he has taken a right resolve.

kṣipraṁ bhavati dharmātmā śaśvacchāntiṁ nigacchati
kaunteya pratijānīhi na me bhaktaḥ praṇaśyati ||31||

(31) Soon he becomes virtuous (righteous) and secures lasting peace, O'Kaunteya, know for sure, My devotee does not perish.

māṁ hi pārtha vyapāśritya ye'pi syuḥ pāpayonayaḥ
striyo vaiśyās tathā śūdraste'pi yānti parām gatim ||32||

(32) Seeking refuge in Me O' Partha, even those who are born of the wombs of sin—as well as the women, merchants and *sudras,* they all attain the Supreme state.

kiṁ punarbrāhmaṇāḥ puṇyā bhaktā rājarṣayas tathā
anityam asukhaṁ lokam imaṁ prāpya bhajasva mām ||33||

(33) How much more then the holy brahmins and the devoted royal sages; therefore, having come to this transitory, sorrowful world, devote yourself in worship to Me.

manmanā bhava madbhakto madyājī māṁ namaskuru
māmevaiṣyasi yuktvaivamātmānaṁ matparāyaṇaḥ ||34||

(34) Fix your mind on Me, be devoted to Me,

adore Me, salute Me in reverence; thus being united in Yoga with Me and taking Me as your ultimate goal, surely you will come to Me.

'AUM TAT SAT'—Thus, in the Upanishad of the glorious Bhagawad Geeta, the science of the Brahman (Absolute) the scripture of yoga, the dialogue between Srī Kṛṣṇa and Arjuna—thus, ends the chapter nine entitled "Rajavidya-Rajaghuyayoga".

Chapter Ten

VIBHUTIYOGA

THE YOGA OF THE DIVINE MANIFESTATIONS

Śrī Bhagavānuvāca :

bhūya eva mahābāho śṛṇu me paramaṁ vacaḥ

yatte'haṁ prīyamāṇāya vakṣyāmi hitakāmyayā ||1||

The Blessed Lord said :

(1) Once again, O' mighty armed, listen to My Supreme word, since you are very dear to Me, I will speak to you for your welfare.

na me viduḥ suragaṇāḥ prabhavaṁ na maharṣayaḥ

aham ādir hi devānaṁ maharṣīnāṁ ca sarvaśaḥ ||2||

(2) Neither the gods, nor the great seers, know about My origin. I am the prime cause of all the gods as well as of the great seers in every way (in all respects).

yo māmajamanādiṁ ca vetti lokamaheśvaram

asammūḍhaḥ sa martyeṣu sarvapāpaiḥ pramucyate ||3||

(3) He who knows Me as unborn, beginningless and as the Supreme Lord of the universe; he is undeluded among the mortals and is liberated from all sins.

buddhirjñānamasammohaḥ kṣamā satyaṁ damaḥ śamaḥ
sukhaṁ duḥkhaṁ bhavo'bhāvo bhayaṁ cābhayameva ca ||4||
ahinsā samatā tuṣṭistapo dānaṁ yaśo'yaśaḥ
bhavanti bhāvā bhūtānāṁ matta eva pṛthagvidhāḥ ||5||

(4, 5) Intellect, wisdom, undeludedness, forgiveness, truthfulness, self-restraint, self-control, pleasure and pain, being and non-being, fear and fearlessness, non-violence, equanimity, contentment, austerity, charity honour and ignomy—all these various qualities of the beings originate from Me alone.

maharṣayaḥ sapta pūrve catvāro manāvas tathā
madbhāvā mānasā jātā yeṣāṁ loka imāḥ prajāḥ ||6||

(6) The seven great sages, and the more ancient Sanaka etc, and the Manus are possessed of powers like Me and born of My mind; all these creatures in the world have descended from them.

etāṁ vibhūtiṁ yogaṁ ca mama yo vetti tattvataḥ
so'vikampena yogena yujyate nātra sanśayaḥ ||7||

(7) He who knows this divine glory and the yogic power of Mine in essence, becomes established in unshakable yogic communion, there is no doubt about it.

ahaṁ sarvasya prabhavo mattaḥ sarvaṁ pravartate

iti matvā bhajante māṁ budhā bhāvasamanvitāḥ ||8||

(8) I am the source of all, from Me everything proceeds; understanding thus, the men of wisdom worship Me, endowed with devotion.

maccittā madgataprāṇā bodhayantaḥ parasparam

kathayantaśca māṁ nityaṁ tuṣyanti ca ramanti ca ||9||

(9) With their mind absorbed in Me, and their life centred on Me, enlightening each other, always speaking of Me, they ever remain contented and delighted.

teṣāṁ satatayuktānāṁ bhajatāṁ prītipūrvakam

dadāmi buddhiyogaṁ taṁ yena māmupayānti te ||10||

(10) To those who are ever united in devotion, and worship Me with love, I grant that Yoga of integral wisdom by which they attain Me.

teṣāmevānukampārthamahamajñānajaṁ tamaḥ

nāśayāmyātmabhāvastho jñānadīpena bhāsvatā ||11||

(11) For them, out of mere compassion I dwell

in their hearts (self) and destroy the ignorance-born darkness by the luminous lamp of wisdom.

Arjuna Uvāca :

paraṁ brahma paraṁ dhāma pavitraṁ paramaṁ bhavān
puruṣaṁ śāśvataṁ divyamādidevamajaṁ vibhum ||12||

Arjuna said :

(12) Thou are the Supreme Brahman, the Supreme abode, the Supreme purifier, the primordial Divine Purusha, the Primal God, unborn and the omnipresent.

āhus tvām ṛṣayaḥ sarve devarṣir nāradastathā
asito devalo vyāsaḥ svayam caiva bravīṣi me ||13||

(13) All the sages have thus declared of You, as also the celestial sage Narada, so also Asita, Devala and Vyasa, and even You—Yourself are telling this to me.

sarvametad ṛtaṁ manye yanmāṁ vadasi keśava
na hi te bhagavanvyaktiṁ vidur devā na dānavāḥ ||14||

(14) I believe all this to be true which You are telling me O' Kesava, neither the gods nor the demons O' Blessed Lord, know your manifestation.

svayamevātmanātmanaṁ vettha tvaṁ puruṣottama
bhūtabhāvana bhūteśa devadeva jagatpate ||15||

(15) You alone know Yourself, by Yourself, O' Supreme person, O' source and Lord of beings, O' God of gods, O' master of the universe.

vaktumarhasyaśeṣeṇa divyā hyātmavibhūtayaḥ
yābhir vibhūtibhir lokānimāṅs tvaṁ vyāpya tiṣṭhasi ||16||

(16) Therefore, You alone without reserve, can describe in full Your Divine manifestations, by which attributes and glories, You remain pervading in these worlds.

kathaṁ vidyāmahaṁ yogiṅstvāṁ sadā paricintayan
keṣu-keṣu ca bhāveṣu cintyo'si bhagavan mayā ||17||

(17) How may I know You, O' Master of Yoga, while constantly meditating upon You; in what particular form, O' blessed Lord, You are to be meditated upon by me?

vistareṇātmano yagaṁ vibhūtiṁ ca janārdana
bhūyaḥ kathaya tṛptirhi śṛṇvato nāsti me'mṛtam ||18||

(18) Tell me again in full detail, Your power of yoga and Your divine manifestations O' Janardana (O'Kṛṣṇa); for I am not yet satisfied by hearing Your nectar-like words.

Śrī Bhagavānuvāca :
hanta te kathayiṣyāmi divyā hyātmavibhūtayaḥ
prādhānyataḥ kuruśreṣṭha nāstyanto vistarasya me ||19||

The Blessed Lord said :

(19) Yes, I must tell you My Divine manifestations but only the specific ones, O' best of the Kurus, for there is no limit to My magnitude.

aham ātmā guḍākeśa sarvabhūtāśayasthitaḥ
ahamādiśca madhyaṁ ca bhūtānāmanta eva ca ||20||

(20) I am the indwelling-soul, O'Gudakesha, (Arjuna) seated in the hearts of all beings, I am the beginning, the middle, as well as the end of all beings.

ādityānaṁ ahaṁ viṣṇur jyotiṣāṁ raviraṅśumān
marīcir marutāmasmi nakṣatrāṇāmahaṁ śaśī ||21||

(21) Among the Adityas, I am Vishnu, among the luminaries, the radiant Sun, I am Marichi among the Maruts, and the Moon among the stars.

vedānāṁ sāmavedo'smi devānāmasmi vasavaḥ
indriyāṇāṁ manaś cāsmi bhūtānāmasmi cetanā ||22||

(22) Of the *Vedas,* I am the *Samaveda;* I am Vasva (Indra), among the gods; among the senses I am the mind; and of the living beings, I am the consciousness.

rudrāṇāṁ śaṅkaraś cā'smi vitteśo yakṣarakṣasām
vasūnāṁ pāvakaścāsmi meruḥ śikhariṇāmaham ||23||

(23) Among the Rudras, I am Sankara, among

the Yakshas and Rakshasa (demons), I am Kubera. Among the Vasus I am the god of fire and of the mountains, I am the Meru.

purodhasāṁ ca mukhyaṁ māṁ viddhi pārtha bṛhaspatim

senānīnāmahaṁ skandaḥ sarasāmasmi sāgaraḥ ||24||

(24) Among the priests, know Me to be their chief, the Brihaspati, O'Partha. Among the army generals, I am Skanda (Kartikeya) and of the reservoirs of water, I am the ocean.

maharṣīṇāṁ bhṛguraham girāmasmyekamakṣaram

yajñānāṁ japayajño'smi sthāvarāṇāṁ himālayaḥ ||25||

(25) Among the great seers, I am Bhrigu; of the words, I am the monosyllable 'AUM'; of yajñas, I am the *Jaap-yajña* (silent repetition of the Lord's name) and among the immovables, the Himalaya.

aśvatthaḥ sarvavṛkṣāṇāṁ devarṣīṇāṁ ca nāradaḥ

gandharvāṇāṁ citrarathaḥ siddhānāṁ kapilo muniḥ ||26||

(26) Among all the trees, I am the Asvattha, among the celestial sages I am Narada, Chitraratha among the gandharvas and among the perfected sages, I am the sage Kapila.

uccaiḥśravasamaśvānāṁ viddhi mām amṛtodbhavam

airāvataṁ gajendrāṇāṁ narāṇāṁ ca narādhipam ||27||

(27) Among the horses know Me to be the

nectar-born celestial horse Ucchaisrava, The Airavata among the lordly elephants and among men the King.

āyudhānāmahaṁ vajraṁ dhenūnām asmi kāmadhuk

prajanaścāsmi kandarpaḥ sarpāṇāmasmi vāsukiḥ ||28||

(28) Of weapons I am the thunderbolt, among cows, I am the celestial wish-yielding cow (Kamadhenu); of the progenitors, I am the God of Love, of the Serpents, I am Vasuki.

anantaścāsmi nāgānāṁ varuṇo yādasāmaham

pitṝṇāmaryamā cāsmi yamaḥ saṅyamatāmaham ||29||

(29) I am Ananta among the snakes and among the aquatic creatures and water gods, I am the Varuna. Among the ancestors, I am the Aryaman and I am Yama among the governors.

prahlādaścāsmi daityānaṁ kālaḥ kalayatāmaham

mṛgāṇāṁ ca mṛgendro'haṁ vainateyaśca pakṣiṇām ||30||

(30) I am Prahlada among the demons; among the reckoners I am Time, among the beasts I am the Lion, and Garuda among the birds.

pavanaḥ pavatāmasmi rāmaḥ śastrabhṛtāmaham

jhaṣāṇāṁ makaraścāsmi srotasāmasmi jāhnavī ||31||

(31) I am the wind among the purifiers (the

speeders), among the wielders of weapons, I am Rama; among the fishes I am alligator and among the rivers I am the holy Ganga.

sargāṇāmādirantaś ca madhyaṁ caivāhamarjuna
adhyātmavidyā vidyānāṁ vādaḥ pravadatāmaham ||32||

(32) Among creations, I am the beginning, the middle, and the end O' Arjuna. Among sciences, I am the science of the Self and the *Vadah* (logic) of those who debate.

akṣarāṇāmakāro'smi dvandvaḥ sāmāsikasya ca
ahamevākṣayaḥ kālo dhātāhaṁ viśvatomukhaḥ ||33||

(33) Of letters I am 'A', of word-compounds, I am the dual, I am verily the imperishable Time; I am the sustainer, facing in all directions.

mṛtyuḥ sarvaharaś cāhamudbhavaś ca bhaviṣyatām
kīrtiḥ śrīr vāk ca nārīṇāṁ smṛtir medhā dhṛtiḥ kṣamā ||34||

(34) I am the all devouring death and the source of things yet to come. Among the feminine virtues I am glory, fortune, speech, memory, wisdom, steadfastness, firmness and forgiveness.

bṛhatsāma tathā sāmnāṁ gāyatrī chandasāmaham
māsānāṁ mārgaśīrṣo'hamṛtūnāṁ kusumākaraḥ ||35||

(35) Of the hymns, I am the *Brihatsaman,*

among the Vedic metres I am the *Gayatri*. Among the months I am Margashirsha, and of seasons the spring.

dyūtaṁ chalayatāmasmi tejaste jasvināmaham
jayo'smi vyavasāyo'smi sattvaṁ sattvavatāmaham ||36||

(36) Of the deceitful, I am the gambling; I am the glory of the glorious and the victory of the victorious. I am determination and the goodness of the good.

vṛṣnīnām vāsudevo'smi pāṇḍavānāṁ dhanañjayaḥ
munīnāmapyahaṁ vyāsaḥ kavīnāmuśanā kaviḥ ||37||

(37) Among the Vrishnis I am Vasudeva; among the Pandavas I am Dhananjaya (Arjuna), I am Vyasa among the sages and among the poets I am Shukracharya.

daṇḍo damayatāmasmi nītirasmi jigīṣatām
maunaṁ caivāsmi guhyānāṁ jñānaṁ jñānavatāmaham ||38||

(38) I am the principle of punishment, of those who punish. I am statesmanship of those who seek victory. Among the secrets I am silence and wisdom of the wise.

yaccāpi sarvabhūtānāṁ bījaṁ tad ahamarjuna
na tadasti vinā yat syān mayā bhūtaṁ carācaram ||39||

(39) I am seed of all living beings O' Arjuna.

There is no being animate or inanimate that can exist without Me.

nānto'sti mama divyānāṁ vibhūtīnāṁ parantapa

eṣa tū'ddeśataḥ prokto vibhūter vistaro mayā ||40||

(40) There is no end of My Divine attributes O' Arjuna. This is only a brief description given by Me of the particulars of My infinite glories.

yad-yad vibhūtimat sattvaṁ śrīmadūrjitameva vā

tat-tad evāvagaccha tvaṁ mama tejoṁśasambhavam ||41||

(41) Every such thing as is glorious, prosperous, powerful, know that to be a manifestation of the fragment of My divine splendour.

athavā bahunaitena kiṁ jñātena tavārjuna

viṣṭabhyāhamidaṁ kṛtsnamekāṅśena sthito jagat ||42||

(42) What is the need of your knowing all these in detail O'Arjuna. I exist supporting the whole universe, with the single fragment of Myself.

'AUM TAT SAT'—Thus, in the Upanishad of the glorious Bhagawad Geeta, the science of the Brahman (Absolute) the scripture of yoga, the dialogue between Srī Kṛṣṇa and Arjuna—thus, ends the chapter ten entitled "Vibhuti-Yoga".

Chapter Eleven

VISVARUPADARSANAYOGA

THE YOGA OF THE VISION OF THE UNIVERSAL FORM

Arjuna Uvāca :

madanugrahāya paramaṁ guhyamadhyātmasañjñitam

yattvayo'ktaṁ vacastena moho'yaṁ vigato mama ||1||

Arjuna said :

(1) By the most profound words of spiritual wisdom which You have spoken out of Your compassion for me, my delusion has been dispelled.

bhavāpyayau hi bhūtānāṁ śrutau vistaraśo mayā

tvattaḥ kamalapatrākṣa māhātmyamapi cāvyayam ||2||

(2) The origin and dissolution of beings have been heard by me in full detail from Thee, O' Lotus-eyed Lord, and also your immortal glory O'Supreme Lord.

evametad yathāttha tvamātmānaṁ parameśvara

draṣṭumicchāmi te rūpam aiśvaraṁ puruṣottama ||3||

(3) You are precisely what you have declared Yourself to be O'Supreme Lord, but I have a desire to see Your Divine form, O' Purushottama (Supreme Purusha).

manyase yadi tacchakyam mayā draṣṭumiti prabho

yogeśvara tato me tvaṁ darśayātmānamavyayam ||4||

(4) O'Lord, if you think that it can be seen by me, then, O'Lord of the Yoga, reveal to me Your imperishable form.

Śrī Bhagavānuvāca :

paśye me pārtha rūpāṇi śataśo'tha sahasraśaḥ

nānāvidhāni divyāni nānāvarṇākṛtīni ca ||5||

The Blessed Lord said :

(5) Behold My forms O'Partha by hundreds and thousands, multifarious and divine, of many colours and shapes.

paśyādityān vasūn rudrān aśvinau marutastathā

bahūny adṛṣṭapūrvāṇi paśyāścāryāṇi bhārata ||6||

(6) Behold the Adityas, the Vasus, the Rudras, the Asvins, and also the Maruts. Behold many more wonders, never seen before, O' Bharta (Arjuna).

ihaikasthaṁ jagat kṛtsnaṁ paśyādya sacarācaram
mama dehe guḍākeśa yaccānyad draṣṭumicchasi ||7||

(7) Now behold within this body of Mine, the whole universe centred in One—the moving and the unmoving, O'Arjuna, and whatever else you desire to see.

na tu māṁ śakyase draṣṭumanenaiva svacakṣuṣā
divyaṁ dadāmi te cakṣuḥ paśya me yogamaiśvaram ||8||

(8) But surely, you cannot see Me with these eyes of yours; therefore, I must bless you with divine vision. Behold My divine power of yoga.

Sañjaya Uvāca :

evamuktvā tato rājan mahāyogeśvaro hariḥ
darśayāmāsa pārthāya paramaṁ rūpamaiśvaram ||9||

Sañjaya said :

(9) After saying this, O' King, the great Lord of Yoga, Hari (Srī Kṛṣṇa) revealed to Arjuna His supreme Divine form.

anekavaktranayanamanekādbhutadarśanam
anekadivyābharaṇaṁ divyānekodyatāyudham ||10||
divyamālyāmbaradharaṁ divyagandhānulepanam
sarvāścaryamayaṁ devamanantaṁ viśvatomukham ||11||

(10, 11) Possessing many mouths and eyes, presenting many wonderful sights, with numerous celestial ornaments and with numerous divine uplifted weapons. Wearing heavenly garlands and garments, anointed all over with divine sandal-pastes; totally marvellous, resplendent, boundless and facing in all directions.

divi sūryasahasrasya bhaved yugapadutthitā
yadi bhāḥ sadṛśī sā syad bhāsas tasya mahātmanaḥ ||12||

(12) If the effulgence of a thousand suns were to blaze forth all at once in the sky, that might resemble the effulgence of that mighty Being.

tatraikasthaṁ jagatkṛtsnaṁ pravibhaktamanekadhā
apaśyad devadevasya śarīre pāṇḍavas tadā ||13||

(13) There, resting at one place in the body of the God of gods, Arjuna then saw the whole universe with its manifold divisions.

tataḥ sa vismayāviṣṭo hṛṣṭaromā dhanañjayaḥ
praṇamya śirasā devaṁ kṛtāñjlirabhāṣata ||14||

(14) Then Arjuna overwhelmed with amazement, his hair standing on end, reverentially bowed down his head before the Lord and spoke with folded hands.

Arjuna Uvāca :

paśyāmi devāns tava deva dehe
sarvāṅs tathā bhūtaviśeṣasaṅghān
brahmāṇamīśaṁ kamalāsanastha-
mṛṣīṅś ca sarvān uragānś ca divyān ||15||

Arjuna said :

(15) O'Lord, I see all the gods in Your body, and also the various multitude of beings; Brahma the Lord seated on His lotus-throne, Shiva and all the other sages and the celestial serpents.

anekabāhūdaravaktranetraṁ
paśyāmi tvāṁ sarvato'nantarūpam
nāntaṁ na madhyaṁ na punastavādiṁ
paśyāmi viśveśvara viśvarūpa ||16||

(16) I see Your infinite form on all sides with numerous arms, stomachs, mouths and eyes. I see neither Your end, nor the middle nor the beginning. O' Lord of the universe, O'cosmic form.

kirīṭinaṁ gadinaṁ cakriṇaṁ ca
tejorāśiṁ sarvato dīptimantam
paśyāmi tvāṁ durnirīkṣyaṁ samantād
dīptānalārkadyutimaprameyam ||17||

(17) I see You with the crown, mace and discus—a mass of radiance shining everywhere; having a brilliance like that of a blazing fire and sun; dazzling and immeasurable on all sides.

tvamakṣaraṁ paramaṁ veditavyaṁ
tvamaśya viśvasya paraṁ nidhānam
tvamavyayaḥ śāśvatadharmagoptā
sanātanas tvaṁ puruṣo mato me ||18||

(18) You are the imperishable, the Supreme being, worthy to be known. You are the ultimate resort of the universe, you are the eternal guardian of the primeval Dharma (Righteousness). You are indeed the primeval Purusha, so I believe.

anādimadhyāntamanantavīrya-
manantabāhuṁ śaśisūryanetram
paśyāmi tvāṁ dīptahutāśavaktram
śvatejasā viśvamidaṁ tapantam ||19||

(19) I see You without beginning, middle or end, of infinite power—with innumerable arms and with the moon and the sun as your eyes. The blazing fire, Your mouth—scorching the universe with your radiance.

dyāvāpṛthivyoridamantaraṁ hi
vyāptaṁ tvayaikena diśaśca sarvāḥ
dṛṣṭvādbhutaṁ rūpamugraṁ tavedaṁ
lokatrayaṁ pravyathitaṁ mahātman ||20||

(20) The space between heaven and earth and in all the quarters is indeed pervaded by You alone. Seeing this most miraculous and dreadful form of Yours, the three worlds are trembling with fear, O' Supreme-soul.

amī hi tvāṁ surasaṁghā viśanti
kecid bhītaḥ prāñjalayo gṛṇanti

svastītyuktvā maharṣisiddhasaṅghāḥ

stuvanti tvāṁ stutibhiḥ puṣkalābhiḥ ||21||

(21) The hosts of gods are entering in You; some in fear with palms joined together are chanting your glories. The multitudes of sages and perfected ones are saying "May it be well" and adore Thee with special hymns of devotional praises.

rudrādityā vasavo ye ca sādhyā

viśve'śvinau marutaś coṣmapāś ca

gandharvayakṣāsursiddhasaṅghā

vīkṣante tvāṁ vismitāś caiva sarve ||22||

(22) The Rudras, Adityas, Vasus, the Sadhyas, Viswas, the Aswins, the Maruts, the manes, the host of Gandharvas, Yakshas, Asuras, and the perfected ones, they are all looking at You in deep amazement.

rūpaṁ mahatte bahuvaktranetraṁ

mahābāho bahubāhūrupādam

bahūdaraṁ bahudaṅṣṭrākarālaṁ

dṛṣṭvā lokāḥ pravyathitāstathāham ||23||

(23) Having seen Thy immeasurable form with numerous mouths, and eyes, O'Kṛṣṇa, with myriad arms and thighs, feet, bellies and fearful teeth, the entire world is in panic, and so am I.

nabhaḥspṛśaṁ dīptamanekavarṇaṁ
vyāttānanaṁ dīptaviśālanetram
dṛṣṭvā hi tvāṁ pravyathitāntarātmā
dhṛtiṁ na vindāmi śamaṁ ca viṣṇo ||24||

(24) When I see Thee touching the sky, blazing with numerous colours, with your mouth wide open and the large shining eyes, my heart trembles with fear and I find neither courage nor peace, O' Lord Vishnu.

daṁṣṭrākarālāni ca te mukhāni
dṛṣṭvaiva kālānalasannibhāni
diśo na jāne na labhe ca śarma
prasīda deveśa jagannivāsa ||25||

(25) Having seen your mouth with fearful teeth, resembling the blazing fire of the cosmic dissolution, I have lost the sense of direction and inner peace. Be gracious O' Lord of the Gods and the abode of the universe.

amī ca tvāṁ dhṛtarāṣṭrasya putrāḥ
sarve sahaivāvanipālasaṅghaiḥ
bhīṣmo droṇaḥ sūtaputrastathāsau
sahāsmadīyairapi yodhamukhyaiḥ ||26||
vaktrāṇi te tvaramāṇā viśanti
daṁṣṭrākarālāni bhayānakāni
kecidvilagnā daśanāntareṣu
saṁdṛśyante cūrṇitairuttamāṅgaiḥ ||27||

(26, 27) All the sons of Dhritarastra with the crowds of other kings, Bhishma, Drona, Karna and with the chief warriors of our side as well, are rushing into your mouths, which is so fearful to look at. Some can be seen sticking in the gaps between the teeth with their heads crushed completely.

yathā nadīnāṁ bahavo'mbuvegāḥ
samudramevā'bhimukhā dravanti
tathā tavāmī naralokavīrā
viśanti vaktrāṇyabhivijvalanti ||28||

(28) As the diverse torrents of rivers rush towards the ocean, similarly these warriors of the mortal world are rushing into Your blazing mouths.

yathā pradīptaṁ jvalanaṁ pataṅgā
viśanti nāśāya samṛaddhavegāḥ
tathaiva nāśāya viśanti lokās
tavāpi vaktrāṇi samṛddhavegāḥ ||29||

(29) As the moths rush into the blazing fire for their own destruction, so also these creatures are hurriedly rushing into Your mouth for their destruction.

lelihyase grasamānaḥ samantāl-
lokān samagrān vadanair jvaladbhiḥ

tejobhirāpūrya jagat samagraṁ

bhāsasta vogrāḥ pratapanti viṣṇo ||30||

(30) Devouring all the worlds on every side with Thy flaming mouths, Your fiery rays are filling the whole world with your effulgence O' Lord Vishnu.

ākhyāhi me ko bhavānugrarūpo

namo'stu te devavara prasīda

vijñātumicchāmi bhavantamādyaṁ

na hi prajānāmi tava pravṛttim ||31||

(31) Tell me who You are in this dreadful form? I bow down to You, O' Supreme Divinity. Be gracious—I want to know You, O'Primal one in reality, for I fail to comprehend Your purpose (intent).

Śrī Bhagavānuvāca :

kālo'smi lokakṣayakṛt pravṛddho

lokān samāhartumiha pravṛttaḥ

ṛte'pi tvāṁ na bhaviṣyanti sarve

ye'vasthitāḥ pratyanīkeṣu yodhāḥ ||32||

The Blessed Lord said :

(32) I am the Time, the mighty world-destroyer; here engaged in the extermination of the worlds. Even without you all these warriors

arrayed in hostile battle will cease to be.

tasmāt tvamuttiṣṭha yaśo labhasva
jitvā śatrūn bhuṅkṣva rājyaṁ samṛddham
mayaivaite nihatāḥ pūrvameva
nimittamātraṁ bhava savyasācin ||33||

(33) Therefore, you stand up, and win the glory. Conquer the enemies and enjoy the unrivalled empire. They have been already killed by Me; you be merely an instrument O' Arjuna.

droṇaṁ ca bhīṣmaṁ ca jayadrathaṁ ca
karṇaṁ tathānyānapi yodhavīrān
mayā hatāṅstvaṁ jahi mā vyathiṣṭhā
yudhyasva jetāsi raṇe sapatnān ||34||

(34) Drona, Bhishma, Jayadrath, Karna and other brave warriors—these have been already killed by Me. Do not be distressed with fear. Fight, you will surely conquer the enemies in the battle.

Sañjaya Uvāca :

etacchrutvā vacanaṁ keśavasya
kṛtāñjalir vepamānaḥ kirīṭī
namaskṛtvā bhūya evāha kṛṣṇaṁ
sagadgadaṁ bhītabhītaḥ praṇamya ||35||

Sanjaya said :

(35) Having heard these words of Srī Kṛṣṇa, Arjuna with his both hands joined together in

respect, trembling and prostrating, once again addressed to Lord Kṛṣṇa in a chocked voice overwhelmed with fear and reverence.

Arjuna Uvāca :

sthāne hṛṣīkeśa tava prakīrtyā

jagat prahṛṣyaty anurajyate ca

rakṣāṅsi bhītāni diśo dravanti

sarve namasyanti ca siddhasaṅghāḥ ||36||

Arjuna said :

(36) O'Kṛṣṇa, right it is that the universe rejoices and is filled with love while glorifying Thee. The terrified demons flee in all directions and all the perfected ones bow to you.

kasmācca te na nameran mahātman

garīyase brahmaṇo'pyādikartre

ananta deveśa jagannivāsa

tvam akṣaraṁ sadasat tat paraṁ yat ||37||

(37) And why should they not salute you O' great Supreme-soul. Thou are the greatest, even greater than Brahma, the original creator. O' Infinite Being, O' God of the gods. Thou are the imperishable, the being, the non-being and that which is beyond both.

tvamādidevaḥ puruṣaḥ purāṇas-

tvamasya viśvasya paraṁ nidhānam

vettā'si vedyaṁ ca paraṁ ca dhāma

tvayā tataṁ viśvam anantarūpa ||38||

(38) You are the Primal God, the most ancient Purusha and the ultimate resort of the universe. You are the knower, the knowable and the Supreme abode. The universe is pervaded by you, O'Lord of infinite forms.

vāyur yamo'gnir varuṇaḥ śaśāṅkaḥ

prajāpatis tvaṁ prapitāmahaśca

namo namaste'stu sahasrakṛtvaḥ

punaśca bhūyo'pi namo namaste ||39||

(39) You are the windgod, the god of death, the god of fire and the god of water, the moongod. You are the creator, the Father of Brahma and the great-grandsire of all. Salutations to You a thousand times; salutations, repeated salutations to You once again.

namaḥ purastād atha pṛṣṭhtaste

namo'stu te sarvata eva sarva

anantavīryāmitvikramas tvaṁ

sarvaṁ samāpnoṣi tato'si sarvaḥ ||40||

(40) Salutation to Thee in front and from

behind, I salute You from all sides, O' infinite in might and infinite in prowess You encompass all, therefore You are all.

sakheti matvā prasabhaṁ yaduktaṁ
he kṛṣṇa he yādava he sakheti
ajānatā mahimānaṁ tavedaṁ
mayā pramādāt praṇayena vāpi ||41||
yaccāvahāsārtham asatkṛto'si
vihārśayyāsanabhojaneṣu
eko'thavā'pyacyuta tatsamakṣaṁ
tatkṣāmaye tvāmahamaprameyam ||42||

(41, 42) Regarding Thee as a friend, I have carelessly addressed You, O' Kṛṣṇa, O' Yadava, O' friend and so on, not knowing Your greatness and magnificence. It has been merely out of my ignorance or affection that You have been slighted by me in jest, while playing, resting or at mealtime, either alone or in the company of others, O'Kṛṣṇa, please forgive me, O' incomprehensible one.

pitāsi lokasya carācarasya
tvamasya pūjyaś ca gururgarīyān
na tvatsamo'sty abhyadhikaḥ kuto'nyo
lokatraye'pyapratimaprabhāva ||43||

(43) You are the Father of the world, moving

and unmoving. You are the most venerable teacher (Guru) and highly adorable. There is no one equal to You in all the three worlds; how can there be any one greater than You. O'Lord of unequalled power.

tasmāt praṇamya praṇidhāya kāyaṁ
prasādaye tvāmahamīśamīḍyam
piteva putrasya sakheva sakhyuḥ
priyaḥ priyāyārhasi deva soḍhum ||44||

(44) Therefore I prostrate before You and request for Your grace O' Lord. As a father forgives his son, a friend to his friend, a lover to his beloved; even so shouldst Thou forgive me, O' Lord.

adṛṣṭapūrvaṁ hṛṣito'smi dṛṣṭvā
bhayena ca pravyathitaṁ mano me
tad eva me darśaya deva rūpaṁ
prasīda deveśa jagannivāsa ||45||

(45) Having seen what was never seen before—I am delighted, but my mind is distressed with fear. Reveal to me, O'God, that other form of Yours. Be gracious, O' Lord of the gods, and abode of the universe.

kirīṭinaṁ gadinaṁ cakrahastam
icchāmi tvāṁ draṣṭumahaṁ tathaiva

tenaiva rūpeṇa caturbhujena

sahasrabāho bhava viśvamūrte ||46||

(46) I desire to see You as before, with Your crown, holding a mace and a discus in your hand. Please resume again that four-armed form, O' thousand-armed, universal Being.

Śrī Bhagavānuvāca :

mayā prasannena tavā'rjune'daṁ

rūpaṁ paraṁ darśitam ātmayogāt

tejomayaṁ viśvamanantamādyaṁ

yanme tvadanyena na dṛṣṭapūrvam ||47||

The Blessed Lord said :

(47) O'Arjuna, being pleased with you I have revealed to you through My power of Yoga, this Supreme, effulgent, infinite, primeval cosmic form of Mine; which no one else has seen before.

na vedayajñādhyayanairna dānair

na ca kriyābhir na tapobhirugraiḥ

evaṁrūpaḥ śakya ahaṁ nṛloke

draṣṭuṁ tvadanyena kurupravīra ||48||

(48) Neither by the study of *Vedas* and yajña, nor by charity, nor by rituals and neither by severe penances, can I be seen in this form in the world

of men by any one else except you, O' hero of the Kurus.

mā te vyathā mā ca vimūḍhabhāvo
dṛṣtvā rūpaṁ ghoramīdṛṅ mamedam
vyapetabhīḥ prītamanāḥ punas tvaṁ
tad eva me rūpamidaṁ prapaśya ||49||

(49) Do not be afraid, nor bewildered, on seeing such an awesome form of Mine. Shedding all your fears and with a gladdened heart, behold once again the other familiar form of Mine.

Sañjaya Uvāca :

ityarjunaṁ vāsudevas tathoktvā
svakaṁ rūpaṁ darśayāmāsa bhūyaḥ
āśvāsayāmāsa ca bhītamenaṁ
bhūtvā punaḥ saumyavapur mahātmā ||50||

Sañjaya said :

(50) Having thus spoken to Arjuna, Lord Vasudeva showed to him again His own form. Assuming His gentle appearance, the exalted one (Srī Kṛṣṇa) comforted and consoled the terrified Arjuna.

Arjuna Uvāca :

dṛṣṭvedaṁ mānuṣaṁ rūpaṁ tava saumyaṁ janārdana
idānīmasmi saṁvṛttaḥ sacetāḥ prakṛtiṁ gataḥ ||51||

Arjuna said :

(51) Having seen this human form of yours which is graciously peaceful O' Kṛṣṇa, now I have regained my composure and am restored to my own natural self again.

Śrī Bhagavānuvāca :

sudurdarśamidaṁ rūpaṁ dṛṣtavānasi yan mama
devā apyasya rūpasya nityaṁ darśanakāṅkṣiṣaḥ ||52||

The Blessed Lord said :

(52) It is indeed very difficult to see this form of Mine which you have just seen. Even the gods are always desirous to behold this form.

nāhaṁ vedairna tapasā na dānena na cejyayā
śakya evaṁvidho draṣṭuṁ dṛaṣṭavān asi māṁ yathā ||53||

(53) Neither by the study of the *Vedas,* nor by penances and charities, nor by rituals, can I be seen in this form as you have seen Me.

bhaktyā tvananyayā śakya ahamevaṁvidho'rjuna
jñātuṁ draṣṭuṁ ca tattvena praveṣṭuṁ ca parantapa ||54||

(54) But only by undivided devotion, however, O' Arjuna, I can be seen in this form, be known in essence and also perceived and experienced.

matkarmakṛn matparamo madbhaktaḥ saṅgavarjitaḥ
nirvairaḥ sarvabhūteṣu yaḥ sa māmeti pāṇḍava ||55||

(55) He who performs all his actions for Me,

considers me as his Supreme goal, and is totally devoted to Me, who is non-attached and free from malice towards all beings, surely comes to Me, O'Arjuna.

'AUM TAT SAT'—Thus, in the Upanishad of the glorious Bhagawad Geeta, the science of the Brahman (Absolute) the scripture of yoga, the dialogue between Srī Kṛṣṇa and Arjuna—thus, ends the chapter eleven entitled "Visvarupadarsanayoga".

Chapter Twelve

BHAKTIYOGA

THE YOGA OF DEVOTION

Arjuna Uvāca :

evaṁ satatayuktā ye bhaktāstvāṁ paryupāsate

ye cāpyakṣaramavyaktaṁ teṣāṁ ke yogavittamāḥ ||1||

Arjuna said :

(1) Those devotees who are ever steadfast and thus worship Thee, and those who worship the imperishable and unmanifested, which of these are better versed in Yoga?

Śrī Bhagavānuvāca :

mayyāveśya mano ye māṁ nityayuktā upāsate

śraddhayā parayo'petās te me yuktatamā matāḥ ||2||

The Blessed Lord said :

(2) Those who concentrate their mind on Me, stay united with Me in contemplation; those are steadfast and worship Me with supreme faith—I

consider them to be the best in Yoga.

ye tvakṣharam anirdeśyamavyaktaṁ paryupāsate

sarvatragamacintyaṁ ca kūṭasthamacalaṁ dhruvam ||3||

saṁniyamyendriyagrāmaṁ sarvatra samabuddhayaḥ

te prāpnuvanti māmeva sarvabhūtahite ratāḥ ||4||

(3, 4) But those who are devoted to the imperishable, the indefinable, the unmanifest, the omnipresent, the unthinkable, the immovable and the eternal; having restrained all their senses in totality, with equanimity of mind, also reach Me, while intent on the welfare of all beings.

kleśo'dhikataras teṣāmavyaktāsaktacetasām

avyaktā hi gatir duḥkhaṁ dehvadbhiravāpyate ||5||

(5) There are greater obstacles for those whose minds are set on the unmanifest; for the goal—the unmanifested is very difficult to attain by the embodied beings.

ye tu sarvāṇi karmāṇi mayi sannyasya matparāḥ

ananyenaiva yogena māṁ dhyāyanta upāsate ||6||

teṣāmahaṁ samuddhartā mṛtyusaṁsārasāgrāt

bhavāmi nacirāt pārtha mayyāveśitacetasām ||7||

(6, 7) But those who worship Me, surrendering all their actions to Me, regarding Me as their supreme goal, meditate on Me with undivided devotion—whose minds are totally absorbed in Me, I become their saviour and liberate them from the ocean of death-bound existence, Oh! Arjuna.

mayyeva mana ādhatsva mayi buddhiṁ niveśaya
nivasiṣyasi mayyeva ata ūrdhvaṁ na saṅśayaḥ ||8||

(8) Settle your mind in Me alone, let your intellect dwell in Me, then you will live in Me alone, there is no doubt about this.

atha cittaṁ samādhātuṁ na śaknoṣi mayi sthiram
abhyāsayogena tato māmicchāptuṁ dhanañjaya ||9||

(9) If, however, you are not able to fix your mind steadily on Me, then through the Yoga of constant practice seek to attain Me, Oh! Arjuna.

abhyāse'pyasamartho'si matkarmaparamo bhava
madarthamapi karmāṇi kurvan siddhimavāpsyasi ||10||

(10) If you are not capable of such practice, be thou intent on doing work for My sake, even by performing actions for My sake you will attain perfection.

athaitadapyaśakto'si kartuṁ madyogamāśritaḥ
sarvakarmaphalatyāgaṁ tataḥ kuru yatātmavān ||11||

(11) If you are unable to do even this, then

take refuge in My yogic unity and renounce the fruit of all actions, being self-controlled.

śreyo hi jñānamabhyāsājjñānād dhyānaṁ viśiṣyate
dhyānāt karmaphalatyāgas tyāgācchāntiranantaram ||12||

(12) Better indeed is knowledge than practice, (without proper insight) better than knowledge is meditation, superior to meditation is renunciation of the fruits of actions—from renunciation one attains peace immediately.

adveṣṭā sarvabhūtānāṁ maitraḥ karuṇa eva ca
nirmamo nirahaṅkāraḥ samduḥkhasukhaḥ kṣamī ||13||
santuṣṭaḥ satataṁ yogī yatātmā dṛḍhaniścayaḥ
mayyarpitamanobuddhir yo madbhaktaḥ sa me priyaḥ ||14||

(13, 14) He who is free from hatred towards all creatures, friendly and compassionate, who is free from the feeling of mineness and egoism, balanced in pain and pleasure, forgiving, always contented, steadfast in Yoga, self-controlled and very determined, with his mind and intellect dedicated to Me—that devotee of Mine is very dear to Me.

yasmān nodvijate loko lokān nodvijate ca yaḥ
harṣāmarṣabhayodvegair mukto yaḥ sa ca me priyaḥ ||15||

(15) He by whom the world is not agitated and who cannot be agitated by the world; who is free from exhilaration, resentment, fear and anxiety—he is dear to Me.

anapekṣah śucir dakṣa udāsīno gatavyathaḥ

sarvārambhaparityāgī yo madbhaktaḥ sa me priyaḥ ||16||

(16) He who is free from desires, pure, dexterous, and mature, who is free from disappointments and totally detached from all commencements, that devotee of Mine is very dear to Me.

yo na hṛṣyati na dveṣṭi na śocati na kāṅkṣati

śubhāśubhaparityāgī bhaktimānyāḥ sa me priyaḥ ||17||

(17) He who neither exhilarates nor hates, neither grieves nor craves, who is the renouncer of both auspicious and inauspicious, and also endowed with devotion—he is dear to Me.

samaḥ śatrau ca mitre ca tathā mānāpamānayoḥ

śītoṣṇasukhaduḥkheṣu samaḥ saṅgavivarjitaḥ ||18||

(18) Who is alike to a foe and a friend and also the same in honour and dishonour, cold and heat, pleasure and pain, who is poised and detached.

tulyanindāstutir maunī santuṣṭo yena kenacit

aniketaḥ sthiramatir bhaktimān me priyo naraḥ ||19||

(19) Who remains balanced in criticism and praise and holds control over speech, who is contented with anything that comes and not attached to his place of dwelling; who is firm in mind and fully devoted—that man is dear to Me.

ye tu dharmyāmṛtamidaṁ yathoktaṁ paryupāsate

śraddadhānā matparamā bhaktās te'tīva me priyāḥ ||20||

(20) Those who follow this immortal Dharma as declared above, endowed with faith, who regard Me as their supreme goal, those devotees are exceedingly dear to Me.

'AUM TAT SAT'—Thus, in the Upanishad of the glorious Bhagawad Geeta, the science of the Brahman (Absolute) the scripture of yoga, the dialogue between Srī Kṛṣṇa and Arjuna—thus, ends the chapter twelve entitled "Bhaktiyoga".

Chapter Thirteen

KṢETRAKṢETRAJÑA VIBHĀGAYOGA

THE YOGA OF THE KNOWLEDGE OF THE FIELD AND THE KNOWER OF THE FIELD

Śrī Bhagavānuvāca :

idaṁ śarīraṁ kaunteya kṣetramityabhidhīyate

etad yo vetti taṁ prāhuḥ kṣetrajña iti tadvidaḥ ||1||

The Blessed Lord said :

(1) This body O' Arjuna is called the field and he, who knows this, is called the knower of the field by the Sages.

kṣetrajñaṁ cāpi māṁ viddhi sarvakṣetreṣu bhārata

kṣetrakṣetrajñayor jñānaṁ yat tajjñānaṁ mataṁ mama ||2||

(2) Know Me as the knower of the field in all fields, O' Arjuna. The knowledge of the field and the knower of the field is considered to be the true knowledge by Me.

tat kṣetraṁ yācca yādṛk ca yadvikāri yataśca yat

sa ca yo yatprabhāvaś ca tat samāsena me śṛṇu ||3||

(3) That field, what it is like, and what are its modifications and whence it is, also who is the knower of the field and what are his powers—hear all that from Me in brief.

ṛṣibhirbahudhā gītaṁ chandobhir vividhaiḥ pṛthak

brahmasūtrapadaiś caiva hetumadbhir viniścitaiḥ ||4||

(4) The sages have sung about this very distinctively in Vedic hymns with multifold descriptions and also in the conclusive and reasoned text of the *Brahma-sutras.*

mahābhūtānyahaṅkāro buddhiravyaktameva ca

indriyāṇi daśaikaṁ ca pañca cendriyagocarāḥ ||5||

icchā dveṣaḥ sukhaṁ duḥkhaṁ saṁghātaś cetanā dhṛtiḥ

etat kṣetraṁ samāsena savikāramudāhṛtam ||6||

(5, 6) The great elements, the ego, intellect, unmanifested primordial Nature, the ten senses, alongwith mind and five objects of senses. Desire, aversion, pleasure and pain, body, consciousness, fortitude—this is the field with its modifications described briefly.

amānitvam adambhitvamahiṁsā kṣāntirārjavam

ācāryopāsanaṁ śaucaṁ sthairyamātmavinigrahaḥ ||7||

indriyārtheṣu vairāgyamanahaṅkāra eva ca

janmamṛtyujarāvyadhiduḥkhadoṣānudarśanam ||8||

(7, 8) Absence of vanity, unpretentiousness, non-violence, forbearance, uprightness, service to the teacher, purity, steadfastness and self-control. Dispassion towards the objects of the senses, absence of egoism, perception of misery and evil, inherent in birth, death old age and disease.

asaktiranabhiṣvaṅgaḥ putradāragṛhādiṣu

nityam ca samacittatvam iṣṭāniṣṭopapattiṣu ||9||

mayi cānanyayogena bhaktiravyabhicāriṇī

viviktadeśasevitvamaratir janasaṅsadi ||10||

(9, 10) Non-attachment and the attitude of non-possessiveness towards son, wife, home and others. Perennial equal-mindedness on the attainment of all desirable and the undesirable. An undivided devotion for Me through Yoga of contemplation. Resort to solitary places and avoidance from the mass of people.

adhyātmajñānanityatvaṁ tattvajñānārthadarśanam

etajjñānamiti proktamajñānaṁ yadato'nyathā ||11||

(11) Steadfastness in the knowledge of the Self, clear perception of the aim of true knowledge— All this is declared to be the knowledge and

whatever opposed to this is called ignorance.

jñeyaṁ yat tat pravakṣyāmi yaj jñātvāmṛtamaśnute

anādimat paraṁ brahma na sat tannāsad ucyate ||12||

(12) I shall tell you that which has to be known, and by knowing which one attains immortality; the beginningless Supreme Brahman, which is called neither existent *(sat)* nor non-existent *(asat)*.

sarvataḥ pāṇipādaṁ tat sarvato'kṣiśiromukham

sarvataḥśrutimalloke sarvamāvṛtya tiṣṭhati ||13||

(13) With hands and feet everywhere, with eyes, heads and face on all sides, with ears everywhere He pervades in the worlds enveloping everything.

sarvendriyaguṇābhāsaṁ sarvendriyavivarjitam

asaktaṁ sarvabhṛccaiva nirguṇaṁ guṇabhoktṛ ca ||14||

(14) Perceived through the functions of senses, yet devoid of all senses; unattached yet sustaining all; transcends the qualities of nature yet their experiencer.

bahirantaś ca bhūtānāmacaraṁ carameva ca

sūkṣmatvāt tad avijñeyaṁ dūrasthaṁ cāntike ca tat ||15||

(15) Exists without and within all beings, the unmoving and also the moving. Extremely subtle and incomprehensible; very far away and yet so near is That.

avibhaktaṁ ca bhūteṣu vibhaktamiva ca sthitam
bhūtabhartṛ ca tajjñeyaṁ grasiṣṇu prabhaviṣṇu ca ||16||

(16) The 'One' which is undivided yet exists as if divided in all beings; known as the sustainer of all beings, and also the devourer and the creator.

jyotiṣāmapi tajjyotis tamasaḥ param ucyate
jñānaṁ jñeyaṁ jñānagamyaṁ hṛdi sarvasya viṣṭhitam ||17||

(17) That, the Light of all lights, is said to be beyond darkness: The knowledge, the object of knowledge, as well as the goal of knowledge is seated in the hearts of all.

iti kṣetraṁ tathā jñānaṁ jñeyaṁ coktaṁ samāsataḥ
madbhakta etad vijñāya madbhāvāyopapadyate ||18||

(18) Thus the field, the knowledge and the knowable have been illustrated briefly. My devotee who understands all this, he enters into My being.

prakṛtiṁ puruṣaṁ caiva viddhyanādī ubhāvapi
vikārānś ca guṇānś caiva viddhi prakṛtisambhavān ||19||

(19) Know that the Prakriti (Nature) and Purusha (Spirit) are both beginningless; and also understand, that all modifications and the qualities are born of Nature.

kārya karaṇa kartṛtve hetuḥ prakṛtirucyate
puruṣaḥ sukhaduḥkhānāṁ bhoktṛtve heturucyate ||20||

(20) The Primordial Nature is considered to be the cause of effect, instrument and agent; while the embodied-soul is said to be the cause in regard to the experience of pleasure and pain.

puruṣaḥ prakṛtistho hi bhuṅkte prakṛtijān guṇān
kāraṇaṁ guṇasaṅgo'sya sadasadyo nijanmasu ||21||

(21) The soul while settled in identification with Nature experiences the qualities born of nature; it is the attachment to these qualities that becomes the cause of birth in good and evil wombs.

upadraṣṭānumantā ca bhartā bhoktā maheśvaraḥ
paramātmeti cāpyukto dehe'smin puruṣaḥ paraḥ ||22||

(22) The Supreme spirit while dwelling in this body is also called the spectator, the counsellor, the sustainer, the experiencer, the great Lord and the Supreme-Self.

ya evaṁ vetti puruṣaṁ prakṛtiṁ ca guṇaiḥ saha
sarvathā vartamāno'pi na sa bhūyo'bhijāyate ||23||

(23) He who thus knows the Purusha (soul) as well as the Prakriti (Nature) with the qualities (attributes); even though engaged in all respects, he is not born again.

dhyānenātmani paśyanti kecid ātmānamātmanā
anye sāṅkhyena yogena karmayogena cāpare ||24||

(24) Some, by meditation, perceive the Self, in the self, by the self; others by the Yoga of knowledge, and still others by the Yoga of action.

anye tvevamajānantaḥ śrutvānyebhya upāsate
te'pi cātitarantyeva mṛtyuṁ śrutiparāyaṇaḥ ||25||

(25) Others, not knowing thus; worship as they have heard from others; they too cross beyond death, by being devoted to whatever they hear respectfully.

yāvat sañjāyate kiñcit sattvaṁ sthāvarajaṅgamam
kṣetrakṣetrajñasaṁyogāt tad viddhi bharatarṣabha ||26||

(26) Whatever being is born, moving or unmoving, know that it is through the union of the field and the knower of the field, O' best of the Bharatas.

samaṁ sarveṣu bhūteṣu tiṣṭhantaṁ parameśvaram
vinaśyatsvavinaśyantaṁ yaḥ paśyati sa pasyati ||27||

(27) He who beholds the Supreme Lord existing equally in all beings, as the imperishable within the perishable, he truly sees.

samaṁ paśyan hi sarvatra samavasthitamīśvaram
na hinstyātmanātmānaṁ tato yāti parāṁ gatim ||28||

(28) Who sees the Supreme Lord present,

equally everywhere, he does not destroy the Self by the self; therefore, he attains the Supreme goal.

prakṛtyaiva ca karmāṇi kriyamāṇāni sarvaśaḥ

yaḥ paśyati tathātmānamakartāraṁ sa paśyati ||29||

(29) He who sees, that all the actions are being performed by Prakriti (Nature) and the Self is not the doer, he truly sees.

yadā bhūtapṛthagbhāvamekasthamanupaśyati

tata eva ca vistāraṁ brahma saṁpadyate tadā ||30||

(30) When he sees, that the whole variety of beings are centred in 'One' and their expansion is from that 'One' alone, then he attains Brahman.

anāditvānnirguṇatvāt paramātmāyamavyayaḥ

śarīrastho'pi kaunteya na karoti na lipyate ||31||

(31) Beginningless, and beyond the qualities of Nature, the Supreme-Self is imperishable. Although existing in the body O' Arjuna, neither acts nor is attached.

yathā sarvagataṁ saukṣmyād ākāśaṁ nopalipyate

sarvatrāvasthito dehe tathātmā nopalipyate ||32||

(32) As the all-pervading ether is not tainted, because of its subtlety, even so the Self, although dwelling everywhere in the body, is not tainted.

yathā prakaśayatyekaḥ kṛtsnaṁ lokamimaṁ raviḥ

kṣetraṁ kṣetrī tathā kṛtsnaṁ prakāśayati bhārata ||33||

(33) As the one sun illuminates the whole universe, so also the Lord of the field illuminates the entire field, O'Arjuna.

kṣetrakṣetrajñayorevamantaraṁ jñānacakṣuṣā
bhūtaprakṛtimokṣaṁ ca ye vidur yānti te param ||34||

(34) Those, who perceive the distinction between the field and the knower of the field with the eye of wisdom; and the deliverance of beings from *Prakriti* (Nature), they attain the Supreme.

'AUM TAT SAT'—Thus, in the Upanishad of the glorious Bhagawad Geeta, the science of the Brahman (Absolute) the scripture of yoga, the dialogue between Srī Kṛṣṇa and Arjuna—thus, ends the chapter thirteen entitled "Ksetraksetrajña-vibhagayoga".

Chapter Fourteen

GUNATRIYA VIBHAGAYOGA

THE YOGA OF THE DIVISION OF THE THREE GUNAS

Śrī Bhagavānuvāca :

paraṁ bhūyaḥ pravakṣyāmi jñānānāṁ jñānamuttamam

yajjñātvā munayaḥ sarve parāṁ siddhim ito gatāḥ ||1||

The Blessed Lord said :

(1) I shall teach you again the supreme knowledge, the highly reverend knowledge; by knowing which, all the sages have attained the supreme perfection, being liberated from the world.

idaṁ jñānamupāśritya mama sādharmyamāgatāḥ

sarge'pi nopajāyante pralaye na vyathanti ca ||2||

(2) Those who have taken refuge in this knowledge, have attained unity with Me. They are not born at the time of creation, nor are they disturbed at the time of dissolution.

mama yonir mahad brahma tasmin garbhaṁ dadhāmyaham
sambhavaḥ sarvabhūtānāṁ tato bhavati bhārata ||3||

(3) The great Brahma (primordial nature) is My womb; in that, I place the seed, from that, is the birth of all beings O'Arjuna.

sarvayoniṣu kaunteya mūrtayaḥ sambhavanti yāḥ
tāsāṁ brahma mahad yoniraham bījapradaḥ pitā ||4||

(4) Of all the bodies, those take birth from different wombs, O' Arjuna—the great Brahma (Mother nature) is their womb and I am the seed giving Father.

sattvaṁ rajas tama iti guṇāḥ prakṛtisambhavāḥ
nibadhnanti mahābāho dehe dehinamavyayam ||5||

(5) *Sattva* (purity), *Rajas* (passion) and *Tamas* (dullness)—these qualities born of Nature O'Arjuna, bind the imperishable spirit to the body.

tatra sattvaṁ nirmalatvāt prakāśakamanāmayam
sukhasaṅgena badhnāti jñānasaṅgena cānagha ||6||

(6) Of these *Sattva* (purity) being immaculate, luminous and healthy binds by attachment to happiness and by attachment to knowledge, O' Arjuna.

rajo rāgātmakaṁ viddhi tṛṣṇāsaṅgasamudbhavam
tannibadhnāti kaunteya karmasaṅgena dehinam ||7||

(7) Know thou, *Rajas* to be of the nature of passion, which is the source of thirst and attachment; it binds O'Kaunteya, the embodied-self through attachment to action.

tamastvajñānajaṁ viddhi mohanaṁ sarvadehinām

pramādālasyanidrābhis tannibadhnāti bhārata ||8||

(8) Know, *Tamas* to be born of ignorance, it deludes the embodied beings and binds through negligence, indolence and sleep O' Arjuna.

sattvaṁ sukhe sañjayati rajaḥ karmaṇi bhārata

jñānamāvṛtya tu tamaḥ pramāde sañjayatyuta ||9||

(9) The mode of *Sattva* binds one with attachment to happiness, *Rajas* attaches one with obsession to work O'Arjuna, while *Tamas* veiling the knowledge attaches one to heedlessness and laziness.

rajas tamaś cābhibhūya sattvaṁ bhavati bhārata

rajaḥ sattvaṁ tamaś caiva tamaḥ sattvaṁ rajastathā ||10||

(10) *Sattva* prevails having overpowered *Rajas* and *Tamas,* O'Arjuna. *Rajas* prevails having overpowered *Sattva* and *Tamas* and likewise *Tamas* manifests overpowering *Sattva* and *Rajas.*

sarvadvāreṣu dehe'smin prakāśa upajāyate

jñānaṁ yadā tadā vidyād vivṛddhaṁ sattvamityuta ||11||

(11) When through every gate of the body, the light of wisdom shines forth, then it may be understood that *Sattva* is predominant.

lobhaḥ pravṛttirārambhaḥ karmaṇāmaśamaḥ spṛhā

rajasyetāni jāyante vivṛddhe bharatarṣabha ||12||

(12) Covetousness, activity, enterprise, restlessness and craving—these arise when *Rajas* is predominant, O'Arjuna.

aprakāśo'pravṛttiś ca pramādo moha eva ca

tamasyetāni jāyante vivṛddhe kurunandana ||13||

(13) Darkness, lack of effort, negligence and mere delusion—these arise when *Tamas* is predominant, O'Arjuna.

yadā sattve pravṛddhe tu pralayaṁ yāti dehabhṛt

tadottamavidāṁ lokānamalān pratipdyate ||14||

(14) When the embodied-self meets death, while *Sattva* is predominant, then he attains to the pure world of the knowers of the highest.

rajasi pralayaṁ gatvā karmasaṅgiṣu jāyate

tathā pralīnas tamasi mūḍhayoniṣu jāyate ||15||

(15) When the individual dies with the predominance of *Rajas,* he is born among those who are attached to action. Meeting death in *Tamas,* he is born in the wombs of the deluded.

karmaṇaḥ sukṛtasyāhuḥ sāttvikaṁ nirmalaṁ phalam

rajasas tu phalaṁ duḥkhamajñānaṁ tamasaḥ phalam ||16||

(16) The fruit of good action is *Sattvic* and pure; while the fruit of *Rajas* is pain and sorrow—ignorance is the fruit of *Tamas*.

sattvāt sañjāyate jñānaṁ rajaso lobha eva ca

pramādamohau tamaso bhavato'jñānameva ca ||17||

(17) *Sattva* promotes knowledge and *Rajas* promotes greed, while heedlessness and delusion arise from *Tamas* and also the ignorance.

ūrdhvaṁ gacchanti sattvasthā madhye tiṣṭhanti rājasāḥ

jaghanyaguṇavṛttisthā adho gacchanti tāmasāḥ ||18||

(18) Those who are settled in *Sattva* go upward. The *Rajasic* dwell in the middle and the *Tamasic* remaining under the influence of the lowest qualities go downward.

nānyaṁ guṇebhyaḥ kartāraṁ yadā draṣṭānupaśyati

guṇebhyaś ca paraṁ vetti madbhāvaṁ so'dhigacchati ||19||

(19) When the seer beholds no agent other than the qualities of nature, and perceives the transcendent beyond the qualities, he attains to My being.

guṇān etānatītya trīn dehī dehasamudbhavān

janmamṛtyujarāduḥkhair vimukto'mṛtamaśnute ||20||

(20) When the embodied-self transcends the three Gunas, out of which the body is evolved, then he is released from birth, death, old age and misery; he attains immortality.

Arjuna Uvāca :

kair liṅgais trīn guṇānetānatīto bhavati prabho

kimācāraḥ kathaṁ caitāṅs trīn gunānativartate ||21||

Arjuna said :

(21) What are the hallmarks of the man, who has transcended the three Gunas, O'Lord? What is his conduct, and how does he transcend the three Gunas (qualities)?

Śrī Bhagavānuvāca :

prakāśaṁ ca pravṛttiṁ ca mohameva ca pāṇḍava

na dveṣṭi saṁpravṛttāni na nivṛttāni kāṅkṣati ||22||

The Blessed Lord said :

(22) When there is enlightenment, activity and delusion in life O'Arjuna, he does not dislike them; nor does he long for them when they are absent.

udāsīnavadāsīno guṇair yo na vicālyate

guṇā vartanta ityeva yo'vatiṣṭhati neṅgate ||23||

(23) He, who remains unconcerned and does not feel disturbed by these qualities; he acts merely as a witness. He understands that only the Gunas

are in operation, so he remains firm and established in the Self.

samaduḥkhasukhaḥ svasthaḥ samaloṣṭāśmakāñcanaḥ

tulyapriyāpriyo dhīras tulyanindātmasaṁstutiḥ ||24||

(24) He, who is balanced in pain and pleasure and remains centred in the Self; who looks upon a clod, a stone, and a piece of gold as of equal worth, who remains balanced amidst the pleasant and the unpleasant, who is steadfast and regards both blame and praise of himself as equal.

mānāpamānayostulyas tulyo mitrāripakṣayoḥ

sarvārambhaparityāgī guṇātītaḥ sa ucyate ||25||

(25) Who maintains his balance in honour and dishonour, who is equal to a friend and foe, who is detached in all undertakings—he is said to have transcended the Gunas (qualities).

māṁ ca yo'vyabhicāreṇa bhaktiyogena sevate

sa guṇān samatītyaitān brahmabhūyāya kalpate ||26||

(26) Who serves Me with an undeviated Yoga of devotion, he rises above the Gunas and becomes fit, to be one with Brahman.

brahmaṇo hi pratiṣṭhāham amṛtasyāvyayasya ca

śāśvatasya ca dharmasya sukhasyaikāntikasya ca ||27||

(27) For, I am the abode of Brahman, the immortal and the imperishable, of the primordial

eternal Dharma and of Absolute Bliss.

'AUM TAT SAT'—Thus, in the Upanishad of the glorious Bhagawad Geeta, the science of the Brahman (Absolute) the scripture of yoga, the dialogue between Srī Kṛṣṇa and Arjuna—thus, ends the chapter fourteen entitled "Gunatriya-vibhagayoga".

Chapter Fifteen

PURUSHOTTAMAYOGA

THE YOGA OF THE SUPREME PERSON

Śrī Bhagavānuvāca :

ūrdhvamūlamadhaḥśākham aśvatthaṁ prāhuravyayam

chandānsi yasya parṇāni yas taṁ veda sa vedavit ||1||

The Blessed Lord said :

(1) Having its roots above and branches below, the *asvattha,* tree is known to be indestructible. Its leaves are the Vedic hymns (metres); he who knows it, is the knower of the Vedas.

adhaścordhvaṁ prasṛtās tasya śākhā

guṇapravṛddhā viṣayapravālāḥ

adhaś ca mūlānyanusantatāni

karmānubandhīni manuṣyaloke ||2||

(2) Its branches extend below and above, nourished by the Gunas. The objects of the senses are the shoots and its rootings are stretched forth—below in the world of men, resulting in the bondage of actions.

na rūpamasyeha tathopalabhyate

nānto na cādirna ca sampratiṣṭhā

aśvatthamenaṁ suvirūḍhamūlam

asaṅgaśastreṇa dṛḍhena chittvā ||3||

(3) Its real form is not thus perceived here, neither its end, nor its origin, nor its foundation; having cut off this deep-rooted tree with the strong axe of non-attachment.

tataḥ padaṁ tat parimārgitavyaṁ

yasmin gatā na nivartanti bhūyaḥ

tameva cādyaṁ puruṣaṁ prapadye

yataḥ pravṛttiḥ prasṛtā purāṇī ||4||

(4) Then, that highest goal should be pursued, whither having reached no one returns again. Saying "I seek refuge in the primordial Purusha, from whom has streamed forth this ancient current of the world".

nirmānamohā jitasaṅgadoṣā

adhyātmanityā vinivṛttakāmāḥ

dvandvairvimuktāḥ sukhaduḥkhasañjñair

gacchantyamūḍhāḥ padamavyayaṁ tat ||5||

(5) Free from egoism and delusion, victorious over the evils of attachment, perennially absorbed in the study of the Self; totally free from desires and the pairs of opposites such as pleasure and

pain, the undeluded reach the eternal state.

na tad bhāsayate sūryo na śaśāṅko na pāvakaḥ
yad gatvā na nivartante tad dhāma paramaṁ mama ||6||

(6) Neither the sun, nor the moon, nor the fire illuminates that; having reached there, they do not return that is My Supreme Abode.

mamaivāṅśo jīvaloke jīvabhūtaḥ sanātanaḥ
manaḥṣaṣṭhānīndriyāṇi prakṛtisthāni karṣati ||7||

(7) An eternal fragment of Myself, having become the embodied-soul in the world of living; draws to itself the senses with the mind as the sixth, which rests in Prakriti (Nature).

śarīraṁ yad avāpnoti yaccāpyutkrāmatīśvaraḥ
gṛhītvaitāni saṅyāti vāyur gandhānivaśayāt ||8||

(8) When the soul (as embodied-soul) takes up a body and also when he leaves it, he takes along these (the mind and senses) and goes as the wind carries the perfumes from their seats.

śrotraṁ cakṣuḥ sparśanaṁ ca rasanaṁ ghrāṇameva ca
adhiṣṭhāya manaścāyaṁ viṣayānupasevate ||9||

(9) Presiding over the ears, the eyes, the touch, taste and smell as well as the mind; the embodied-soul enjoys the object of the senses.

utkrāmantaṁ sthitaṁ vāpi bhuñjānaṁ vā guṇānvitaṁ
vimūḍhā nānupaśyanti paśyanti jñānacakṣuṣaḥ ||10||

(10) The deluded do not perceive the indwelling-soul, while departing from or dwelling in the body and experiencing the objects of the senses in contact with the modes; but they who possess the eye of wisdom truly see.

yatanto yoginaś cainaṁ paśyantyātmanyavasthitam
yatanto'pyakṛtātmāno nainaṁ paśyanty acetasaḥ ||11||

(11) The striving yogins do perceive the indwelling-soul, established in the Self but the ignorant those have not purified their hearts; even though endeavouring, do not perceive the indweller.

yadādityagataṁ tejo jagad bhāsayate'khilam
yaccandramasi yaccāgnau tat tejo viddhi māmakam ||12||

(12) The light of the sun which illumines the whole universe, that which is also in the moon and fire—know that light to be My splendour.

gāmāviśya ca bhūtāni dhārayāmyaham ojasā
puṣṇāmi cauṣadhīḥ sarvāḥ somo bhūtvā rasātmakaḥ ||13||

(13) Penetrating the earth I support all beings with my vital energy and nourish all the herbs by becoming the sapful soma (moon).

ahaṁ vaiśvānaro bhūtvā prāṇināṁ deham āśritaḥ
prāṇāpānasamāyuktaḥ pacāmyannaṁ caturvidham ||14||

(14) I am the universal fire (vaishvanara) dwelling in the body of all living beings; and joined

with the rhythm of inhalation and exhalation I digest the four kinds of food.

sarvasya cāhaṁ hṛdi sanniviṣṭo
mattaḥ smṛtir jñānamapohanaṁ ca
vedaiś ca sarvairahameva vedyo
vedāntakṛd vedavideva cāham ||15||

(15) I am seated in the hearts of all. I am the source of memory, wisdom and ratiocinative faculty. I am subject to be known through all the *Vedas* : I am the author of Vedanta, as well as the knower of the *Vedas.*

dvāvimau puruṣau loke kṣaraś cākṣara eva ca
kṣaraḥ sarvāṇi bhūtāni kūṭastho'kṣara ucyate ||16||

(16) There are two kinds of purushas in this world, the perishable and the imperishable. All beings are perishable—The unchanging (the soul) is called the imperishable.

uttamaḥ puruṣas tvanyaḥ paramātmetyudāhṛtaḥ
yo lokatrayamāviśya bibhartyavyaya īśvaraḥ ||17||

(17) The Supreme Purusha is yet other than these—called the highest Self; the indestructible Lord. Who enters the three worlds, upholds and sustains them.

yaśmāt kṣaramatīto'hamakṣarādapi cottamaḥ
ato'smi loke vede ca prathitaḥ puruṣottamaḥ ||18||

(18) Since I transcend the perishable and am even higher than the imperishable; therefore in this world as well as in *Vedas,* I am declared to be the Supreme Purusha.

yo māmevamasammūḍho jānāti puruṣottamaṁ
sa sarvavid bhājati māṁ sarvabhāvena bhārata ||19||

(19) The undeluded one, who knows Me thus, as the Supreme Purusha, is the knower of all. He worships Me with his whole being (whole heartedly) O' Arjuna.

iti guhyatamaṁ śāstramidamuktaṁ mayānagha
etad buddhvā buddhimān syāt kṛtakṛtyaś ca bhārata ||20||

(20) Thus, this most profound teaching has been imparted by Me, O'sinless one; by understanding this, one becomes self-enlightened and his goal in life is accomplished, O'Arjuna.

'AUM TAT SAT'—Thus, in the Upanishad of the glorious Bhagawad Geeta, the science of the Brahman (Absolute) the scripture of yoga, the dialogue between Srī Kṛṣṇa and Arjuna—thus, ends the chapter fifteen entitled "Purushottamayoga".

Chapter Sixteen

THE DEVASURSAMPATTI VIBHAGYOGA

THE YOGA OF THE DISTINCTION BETWEEN THE DIVINE AND THE DEMONIACAL ENDOWMENTS

Śrī Bhagavānuvāca :

abhayaṁ sattvasaṅśuddhir jñānayogavyavasthitiḥ

dānaṁ damaśca yajñaś ca svādhyāyas tapa ārjavam ||1||

The Blessed Lord said :

(1) Fearlessness, purity of heart, steadfastness in Yoga of knowledge, charity, self-control, performance of yajña, study of the scriptures, austerity and straightforwardness.

ahimsā satyamakrodhas tyāgaḥ śāntirapaiśunaṁ

dayā bhūteṣvaloluptvaṁ mārdavaṁ hrīracāpalaṁ ||2||

(2) Non-violence, truthfulness, absence of anger, renunciation, peacefulness, aversion to fault

finding, compassion towards all beings, non-covetousness, gentleness, modesty and absence of fickleness.

tejaḥ kṣamā dhṛtiḥ śaucamadroho nātimanitā

bhavanti sampadaṁ daivīmabhijātasya bhārata ||3||

(3) Brilliance, forgiveness, fortitude, purity, absence of hatred, absence of arrogance—These are the marks of the one who is endowed with divine nature, O'Arjuna.

dambho darpoabhimānaś ca krodhaḥ pāruṣyameva ca

ajñānaṁ cābhijātasya pārtha saṁpadamāsurīṁ ||4||

(4) Hypocrisy, arrogance, self-conceit, anger, rudeness and ignorance are the characteristics of the one who is endowed with demoniac nature O'Arjuna.

daivī saṁpad vimokṣāya nibandhāyāsurī matā

mā śucaḥ saṁpadaṁ daivīm abhijāto'si pāṇḍava ||5||

(5) The divine nature is conducive to emancipation and the demoniac to bondage. Grieve not, O'Arjuna, thou art born with divine endowments.

dvau bhūtasargau loke'smindaiva āsura eva ca

daivo vistaraśaḥ prokta āsuraṁ pārtha me śṛṇu ||6||

(6) There are two types of beings in the world: The divine and the demoniac. The divine has been explained in detail, now hear about the demoniac from Me, O'Arjuna.

pravṛttiṁ ca nivṛttiṁ ca janā na vidurāsurāḥ

na śaucaṁ nāpi cācāro na satyaṁ teṣu vidyate ||7||

(7) The demoniac people do not know what to do and what to refrain from; neither purity nor good conduct, nor truth is found in them.

asatyam apratiṣṭhaṁ te jagadāhuranīśvaraṁ

aparasparasambhūtaṁ kimanyat kāmahaitukaṁ ||8||

(8) They say, that the world is without truth, without any foundation and without a God; brought about only by the mutual union with the desire for its cause.

etāṁ dṛṣṭimavaṣṭabhya naṣṭātmāno'lpabuddhayaḥ

prabhavantyugrakarmāṇaḥ kṣayāya jagato'hitāḥ ||9||

(9) Holding fast to this view, these ruined beings of meagre understanding and cruel deeds; come forth as the enemies of the world, for its destruction.

kāmam āśritya duṣpūraṁ dambhamānamadānvitāḥ

mohād gṛhītvāsadgrāhān pravartante'śucivratāḥ ||10||

(10) Filled with insatiable desires, motivated by hypocrisy, vanity and arrogance; they hold false values through delusion and work with impure resolves.

cintāmaparimeyāṁ ca pralayāntāmupāśritāḥ
kāmopabhogaparamā etāvaditi niścitāḥ ||11||

(11) Obsessed with innumerable anxieties, those end only with their death, they regard the enjoyment of sensuous pleasures as their highest goal of life and are fully convinced that, that is all.

āśāpāśaśatairbaddhāḥ kāmakrodhaparāyaṇāḥ
īhante kāmabhogārthamanyāyenārthasañcayān ||12||

(12) Bound by hundreds of fetters of expectations, given over to lust and anger; they strive to collect wealth by illegal means for the gratification of their desires.

idamadya mayā labdhamimaṁ prāpsye manoratham
idam astīdamapi me bhaviṣyati punardhanam ||13||

(13) This has been secured by me today and that desire I must fulfil soon. This wealth is mine, and that wealth will also be mine in future.

asau mayā hataḥ śatrur haniṣye cāparānapi
iśvaroahmahaṁ bhogī siddho'haṁ balovan sukhi ||14||

(14) This enemy has been destroyed by me and others too I will finish soon. I am the master and the enjoyer. I am successful, powerful and very prosperous.

āḍhyo'bhijanavānasmi ko'nyo'sti sadṛśo mayā
yakṣye dāsyāmi modiṣya ityajñānavimohitāḥ ||15||

(15) I am wealthy and born in a noble family. Who else is equal to me? I perform sacrifices, give charity and rejoice; thus they are deluded by ignorance.

anekacittavibhrāntā mohajālasamāvṛtāḥ
prasaktāḥ kāmabhogeṣu patanti narake'śucau ||16||

(16) Bewildered by many fantasies, entangled in the snare of delusion, addicted to the sensual enjoyments, they fall into the foul hell.

ātmasambhāvitāḥ stabdhā dhanamānamadānvitāḥ
yajante nāmayajñais te dambhenāvidhipūrvakam ||17||

(17) Self-conceited, stubborn, intoxicated with arrogance of wealth, they perform sacrifices which are only for name, with ostentation and with disregard to the scriptural ordinance.

ahaṅkāraṁ balaṁ darpaṁ kāmaṁ krodhaṁ ca saṅśritāḥ
māmātmaparadeheṣu pradviṣanto'bhyasūyakāḥ ||18||

(18) Possessed of egoism, power, arrogance, lust and anger, these malicious people despise Me, in their own bodies and in those of others.

tān ahaṁ dviṣataḥ krūrān saṅsāreṣu narādhamān

kṣipāṃyajasramaśubhān āsurīṣveva yoniṣu ||19||

(19) These cruel haters, the most degraded among men in the world; I hurl these evildoers repeatedly into the wombs of demons only.

āsurīṁ yonimāpannā mūḍhā janmani-janmani

māmaprāpyaiva kaunteya tato yāntyadhamāṁ gatim ||20||

(20) Fallen into the wombs of demons, these deluded beings from birth to birth do not attain Me O'Kaunteya. They fall further into the lower state than that.

trividhaṁ narakasyedaṁ dvāraṁ nāśanamātmanaḥ

kāmaḥ krodhas tathā lobhas tasmādetat trayaṁ tyajet ||21||

(21) This is the triple gate of hell, that leads to the destruction of the embodied-self—'Lust, anger and greed'. Therefore, one must abandon these three.

etair vimuktaḥ kaunteya tamodvārais tribhir naraḥ

ācarātyatmanaḥ śreyas tato yāti parāṁ gatim ||22||

(22) The man who is released from these three

gates of darkness O'Arjuna, he practises, what is good for him and thus goes to the highest state.

yaḥ śāstravidhimutsṛjya vartate kāmakārataḥ

na sa siddhimavāpnoti na sukhaṁ na paraṁ gatim ||23||

(23) He who abandons the ordinances of the scriptures and acts merely under the impulse of his desire, he does not attain either perfection, or happiness or the Supreme Goal.

tasmācchāstraṁ pramāṇaṁ te kāryākāryavyavasthitau

jñātvā śāstravidhānoktaṁ karma kartumihārhasi ||24||

(24) Therefore, let the scripture be thy authority, in deciding what ought to be done and what should not to be done; having known what is declared in the ordinance of the scriptures, you should perform your work.

'AUM TAT SAT'—Thus, in the Upanishad of the glorious Bhagawad Geeta, the science of the Brahman (Absolute) the scripture of yoga, the dialogue between Srī Kṛṣṇa and Arjuna—thus, ends the chapter sixteen entitled "Daivasurasampatti-vibhagayoga".

Chapter Seventeen

ŚRADDHĀTRIYA VIBHAGYOGA

THE YOGA OF THE THREEFOLD DIVISION OF THE FAITH

Arjuna Uvāca :

ye śāstravidhimutsṛjya yajante śraddhayānvitāḥ

teṣāṁ niṣthā tu kā kṛṣṇa sattvamāho rajas tamaḥ ||1||

Arjuna said :

(1) Those who, neglecting the ordinances of the scriptures, perform yajña (worship) with faith, what is their status O'Kṛṣṇa? Is it *sattva, rajas* or *tamas*?

Śrī Bhagavānuvāca :

trividhā bhavati śraddhā dehināṁ sā svabhāvajā

sāttvikī rājasī caiva tāmasī ceti tāṁ śṛṇu ||2||

The Blessed Lord said :

(2) The faith of the embodied beings is of three kinds, born of their innate disposition—the

sattvic (pure) the *rajasic* (passionate) and the *tamasic* (ignorant). Thus thou hear of it.

sattvānurūpā sarvasya śraddhā bhavati bhārata
śraddhāmayo'yaṁ puruṣo yo yacchraddhaḥ sa eva saḥ ||3||

(3) The faith of each person is in accordance with his innate nature O'Arjuna. Man is made of his faith; as a man's faith is, so is he.

yajante sāttvikā devān yakṣarakṣāṅsi rājasāḥ
pretān bhūtagaṇānścānye yajante tāmasā janāḥ ||4||

(4) The *sattvic* (pure) men worship the gods; the *rajasic* (passionate) worship the Yakshas and Rakshasas; while others—the *tamasic* (deluded) men worship the ghosts and spirits.

aśāstravihitaṁ ghoraṁ tapyante ye tapo-janāḥ
dambhāhaṅkārsaṁyuktāḥ kāmarāgabalānvitāḥ ||5||

(5) Those men, who practise fierce austerities which are not enjoined by the scriptures, being given to hypocrisy and arrogance, impelled by the force of lust and attachment.

karṣayantaḥ śarīrasthaṁ bhūtagrāmamacetasaḥ
māṁ caivā'ntaḥśarīrasthaṁ tān viddhyāsuraniścayān ||6||

(6) Senselessly torturing all the elements in the body they also hurt Me, who dwells within the body--know them to be of demoniacal resolves.

āhārastvapi sarvasya trividho bhavati priyaḥ

yajñastapas tathā dānaṁ teṣāṁ bhedamimaṁ śṛṇu ||7||

(7) The food, which is liked by everyone, is of three kinds, so is the *yajña,* austerity and charity. Hear thou the distinction of these.

āyuḥ sattvabalārogyasukhaprītivivardhanāḥ

rasyāḥ snigdhāḥ sthirā hṛdyā āhārāḥ sāttvikapriyāḥ ||8||

(8) The foods which promote longevity, purity, strength, health, happiness and cheerfulness, which are tasty, oleaginous, substantial and agreeable are liked by the *sattvic* (pure) people.

kaṭvamlalavaṇātyuṣṇatīkṣṇarūkṣavidāhinaḥ

āhārā rājasasyeṣṭā duḥkhaśokāmayapradāḥ ||9||

(9) The foods which are bitter, sour, saline, excessively hot, pungent, dry and burning are liked by *rajasic;* which cause discomfort, pain and disease.

yātayāmaṁ gatarasaṁ pūti paryuṣitaṁ ca yat

ucchiṣṭamapi cāmedhyaṁ bhojanaṁ tāmasapriyam ||10||

(10) That which is stale, insipid, putrid, discarded and impure is the food liked by the *tamasic.*

aphalākāṅkṣibhir yajño vidhidṛṣṭo ya ijyate

yaṣṭavyameveti manaḥ samādhāya sa sāttvikaḥ ||11||

(11) The *yajña* which is performed selflessly, enjoined by the scriptural ordinance and merely out of the feeling of duty is *sattvic* (pure).

abhisandhāya tu phalaṁ dambhārthamapi caiva yat

ijyate bharataśreṣṭha taṁ yajñaṁ viddhi rājasam ||12||

(12) The *yajña* which is performed, keeping in view its reward and also for the sake of mere display, O'Arjuna, know that to be *rajasic* (passionate).

vidhihīnamasṛṣṭānnaṁ mantrahīnamadakṣiṇam

śraddhāvirahitaṁ yajñaṁ tāmasaṁ paricakṣate ||13||

(13) That which is contrary to the scriptural injunctions and performed without the distribution of food, without chanting the holy hymns, giving gifts and sincere devotion, that *yajña* is said to be *tamasic.*

devadvijaguruprājñapūjanaṁ śaucamārjavam

brahmacaryam ahinsā ca śārīraṁ tapa ucyate ||14||

(14) Worship of the gods, learned men, teachers and men of wisdom; cleanliness, straightforwardness, celibacy and non-violence—are called the austerities of the body.

anudvegakaraṁ vākyaṁ satyaṁ priyahitaṁ ca yat

svādhyāyābhyasanaṁ caiva vāṅmayaṁ tapa ucyate ||15||

(15) The austerity of speech is considered to be the utterance of the words, which do not cause annoyance and are truthful, pleasant and beneficial; also the regular study of *Vedas;* and recitation of the Divine name.

manaḥprasādaḥ saumyatvaṁ maunamātmavinigrahaḥ
bhāvasaṁśuddhirityetat tapo mānasamucyate ||16||

(16) Serenity of mind, gentleness, silence, self-control and total honesty of thoughts—this is called the austerity of the mind.

śraddhayā parayā taptaṁ tapas tat trividhaṁ naraiḥ
aphalākāṅkṣibhir yuktaiḥ sāttvikaṁ paricakṣate ||17||

(17) This threefold austerity, practised with utmost faith by men of steadfast wisdom, without the expectation of a reward, is said to be *sattvic.*

satkāramānapūjārthaṁ tapo dambhena caiva yat
kriyate tadiha proktaṁ rājasaṁ calamadhruvam ||18||

(18) The penance which is practised in order to gain respect, recognition, honour, and with hypocrisy—is said to be *rajasic.* It is unstable and transient.

mūḍhagrāheṇātmano yat pīḍayā kriyate tapaḥ
parasyotsādanārthaṁ vā tat tāmasamudāhṛtam ||19||

(19) The austerity which is practised with deluded understanding and with self-torture or the purpose of causing harm to others, is declared to be *tamasic.*

dātavyamiti yad dānaṁ dīyate'nupakāriṇe
deśe kāle ca pātre ca tad dānaṁ sāttvikaṁ smṛtam ||20||

(20) Charity which is given with a sense of duty to the one from whom nothing is expected in return, and also at the right place and time to a deserving person—that charity has been pronounced as *sattvic.*

yat tu pratyupakārārthaṁ phalamuddiśya vā punaḥ
dīyate ca parikliṣṭaṁ tad dānaṁ rājasaṁ smṛtam ||21||

(21) The gift, which is given with the hope of receiving a favour in return or with the expectation of a reward and also given reluctantly, is considered to be *rajasic.*

adeśakāle yad dānam apātrebhyaś ca dīyate
asatkṛtamavajñātaṁ tat tāmasamudāhṛtam ||22||

(22) The charity that is given at an inappropriate place and time, to an unworthy recipient with disrespect and contempt is declared to be *tamasic.*

oṁ tatsaditi nirdeśo brahmaṇas trividhaḥ smṛtaḥ
brāhmaṇās tena vedāś ca yajñāś ca vihitāḥ purā ||23||

(23) 'Aum Tat Sat'—this has been declared to be the threefold designation of the Brahman; by that, the *Vedas,* the *Brahmanas* and sacrifices were created in the ancient past.

tasmādomityudāhṛtya yajñadanatapaḥkriyāḥ
pravartante vidhānoktāḥ satataṁ brahmavādinām ||24||

(24) Therefore with the utterance of the holy syllable "AUM" the acts of *yajña,* charity and austerity are commenced; as enjoined in the scriptures by the expounders of the *Brahman.*

tadityanabhisandhāya phalaṁ yajñatapaḥkriyāḥ
dānakriyāś ca vividhāḥ kriyante mokṣakāṅkṣibhiḥ ||25||

(25) With the utterance of the word *Tat,* without aiming at the fruit; the various acts of *yajña* (sacrifice) austerity and charity are performed by the seekers of liberation.

sadbhāve sādhubhāve ca sadityetat prayujyate
praśaste karmaṇi tathā sacchabdaḥ pārtha yujyate ||26||

(26) The word *Sat* is used, to express Realty and that which is good. Similarly O'Arjuna, the word *Sat* is used in the sense of an auspicious act.

yajñe tapasi dāne ca sthitiḥ saditi cocyate

karma caiva tadarthīyaṁ sadity evābhidhīyate ||27||

(27) Steadfastness in *yajña* (selfless action) asceticism and charity is also called *Sat;* and also the action which is in connection with these, is called *Sat.*

aśraddhayā hutaṁ dattaṁ tapas taptaṁ kṛtaṁ ca yat

asadityucyate pārtha na ca tat pretya no iha ||28||

(28) Whatever is offered in *yajña,* given as charity, practised as austerity and whatever rite is observed without faith (sincere devotion), is called *asat* O'Arjuna. It bears nothing, neither here nor hereafter.

'AUM TAT SAT'—Thus, in the Upanishad of the glorious Bhagawad Geeta, the science of the Brahman (Absolute) the scripture of yoga, the dialogue between Srī Kṛṣṇa and Arjuna—thus, ends the chapter seventeen entitled "Sraddhatriya-vibhagayoga".

Chapter Eighteen

MOKSASAṄNYASAYOGA

THE YOGA OF LIBERATION THROUGH RENUNCIATION

Arjuna Uvāca :

sannyāsasya mahābāho tattvamicchāmi veditum

tyāgasya ca hṛṣīkeśa pṛthak keśiniṣūdana ||1||

Arjuna Said :

(1) I desire to know in detail the truth about renunciation *(sannyasa)* and also about relinquishment separately, O' Hrishikesa (Srī Kṛṣṇa).

Śrī Bhagavānuvāca :

kāmyānāṁ karmaṇāṁ nyāsaṁ sannyāsaṁ kavayo viduḥ

sarvakarmaphalatyāgaṁ prāhuṣ tyāgaṁ vicakṣaṇāḥ ||2||

The Blessed Lord said :

(2) The sages understand *sannyasa* to be the renunciation of all actions prompted by desire; the learned declare the abandonment of the fruits

of all actions to be the *tyaga* (relinquishment).

tyājyaṁ doṣavadityeke karma prāhur manīṣinaḥ
yajñadānatapaḥ karma na tyājyamiti cāpare ||3||

(3) Some sages declare that actions should be abandoned as an evil, while others say that the act of *yajña* (sacrifice), charity and austerity should not be relinquished.

niścayaṁ śṛṇu me tatra tyāge bharatasattama
tyāgo hi puruṣavyāghra trividhaḥ samprakirtitaḥ ||4||

(4) Listen from Me the final truth about the relinquishment, O'best of the Bharatas (Arjuna). The abandonment, O'best among men, has been declared to be of three kinds.

yajñadānatapaḥ karma na tyājyaṁ kāryameva tat
yajño dānaṁ tapaś caiva pāvanāni manīṣiṇām ||5||

(5) *Yajña* (sacrifice), charity and austerity are not to be abandoned; these should be performed, for the acts of *yajña,* charity and austerity are the purifiers of the wise.

etānyapi tu karmāṇi saṅgaṁ tyaktvā phalāni ca
kartavyānīti me pārtha niścitaṁ matamuttamam ||6||

(6) Even these actions should be performed abandoning all attachments and desire for fruits.

O'Arjuna, this is for certain my decisive opinion.

niyatasya tu sannyāsaḥ karmaṇo nopapadyate
mohāttasya parityāgas tāmasaḥ parikīrtitaḥ ||7||

(7) The renunciation of an obligatory act is not proper; its abandonment through delusion is considered to be *tamasic.*

duḥkhamityeva yat karma kāyakleśabhayāt tyajet
sa kṛtvā rājasaṁ tyāgaṁ naiva tyāgaphalaṁ labhet ||8||

(8) He, who renounces his action, because it is painful or from the fear of physical suffering, his act of renunciation is considered to be *rajasic.* He does not attain the merit of relinquishment.

kāryamityeva yat karma niyataṁ kriyate'rjuna
saṅgaṁ tyaktvā phalaṁ caiva sa tyāgaḥ sāttviko mataḥ ||9||

(9) He, who performs the obligatory actions, simply because it ought to be done; by abandoning attachment and also the desire for the fruit—that relinquishment is regarded to be *sattvic.*

na dveṣṭyakuśalaṁ karma kuśale nānuṣajjate
tyāgī sattvasamāviṣṭo medhāvī chinnasaṅśayaḥ ||10||

(10) The wise man of renunciation is the one who is imbued with the purity of *sattva,* whose doubts are dispelled, who does not hate the

disagreeable work nor is attached to the agreeable one.

na hi dehabhṛtā śakyaṁ tyaktuṁ karmāṇyaśeṣataḥ
yastu karmaphalatyāgī sa tyāgītyabhidhīyate ||11||

(11) Verily, it is not possible for an embodied being to renounce actions altogether. He, who abandons the fruits of actions—he is said to be the renouncer.

aniṣṭamiṣṭaṁ miśraṁ ca trividhaṁ karmaṇaḥ phalam
bhavatyatyāgināṁ pretya na tu sannyāsināṁ kvacit ||12||

(12) Disagreeable, agreeable and mixed—threefold is the fruit of action, accruing after death, to those who have not relinquished—but there is none whatsoever for those who have renounced.

pañcaitāni mahābāho kāraṇāni nibodha me
sāṅkhye kṛtānte proktāni siddhaye sarvakarmaṇām ||13||

(13) Learn from Me, O'mighty armed (Arjuna), these five causes as declared in the *Samkhya* philosophy for the accomplishment of all actions.

adhiṣṭhānaṁ tathā kartā karaṇaṁ ca pṛthagvidham
vividhāś ca pṛthakceṣṭā daivaṁ caivātra pañcamam ||14||

(14) The seat of action (body) and likewise

the doer, the instruments of various sorts (sense organs and mind) many kinds of efforts and providence (destiny) being the fifth.

śarīravāṅgmanobhir yat karma prārabhate naraḥ
nyāyyaṁ vā viparītaṁ vā pañcaite tasya hetavaḥ ||15||

(15) Whatever action a man performs with his body, speech and mind—whether it is right or wrong, these five are its causes.

tatraivaṁ sati kartāramātmānaṁ kevalaṁ tu yaḥ
paśyatyakṛtabuddhitvān na sa paśyati durmatiḥ ||16||

(16) Now, such being the case, the man of impure intellect, who on account of his perverse understanding looks upon himself as the sole agent, he does not see (truly).

yasya nāhaṅkṛto bhāvo buddhiryasya na lipyate
hatvāpi sa imāṅllokān na hanti na nibadhyate ||17||

(17) He, who is free from the egoistic notion of 'I-ness'; and whose mind is not tainted—even though he kills these people, he neither slays nor is he bound.

jñānaṁ jñeyaṁ parijñātā trividhā karmacodanā
karaṇaṁ karma karteti trividhaḥ karmasaṅgrahaḥ ||18||

(18) Knowledge, the object of knowledge, and the knower, form the threefold impulse to action;

the instrument, the action and the agent form the threefold basis of action.

jñānaṁ karma ca kartā ca tridhaiva guṇabhedataḥ

procyate guṇasaṅkhyāne yathāvacchṛṇu tānyapi ||19||

(19) The knowledge, action and the actor are also declared to be threefold, in the science of the gunas, according to the distinction of the gunas. Listen about them also as they are.

sarvabhūteṣu yenaikaṁ bhāvamavyayamīkṣate

avibhaktaṁ vibhakteṣu tajjñanaṁ viddhi sāttvikam ||20||

(20) The knowledge by which one perceives in all beings the 'One' imperishable existence as undivided in the divided—know that knowledge to be *sattvic.*

pṛthaktvena tu yajjñānaṁ nānābhāvān pṛthagvidhān

vetti sarveṣu bhūteṣu tajjñānaṁ viddhi rājasam ||21||

(21) But that knowledge which perceives in all beings, the manifold entities of distinct kind, as different from one another—know that knowledge to be *rajasic.*

yattu kṛtsnavadekasmin kārye saktamahetukam

atattvārthavadalapaṁ ca tat tāmasamudāhṛtam ||22||

(22) That which is confined to one single act, as if it were the whole, which is without reason,

without foundation in truth and is trivial—that is declared to be *tamasic.*

niyataṁ saṅgarahitam arāgadveṣataḥ kṛtam

aphalaprepsunā karma yat tat sāttvikamucyate ||23||

(23) The obligatory action which is performed without attachment, without love or hatred by the one who is not desirous of any reward—that action is called *sattvic.*

yat tu kāmepsunā karma sāhaṅkāreṇa vā punaḥ

kriyate bahulāyāsaṁ tad rājasamudāhṛtam ||24||

(24) That action, however, which is performed with great strain by the one who seeks to gratify his desire or is impelled by egoism—that action is declared to be *rajasic.*

anubandhaṁ kṣayaṁ hinsāmanavekṣya ca pauruṣam

mohād ārabhyate karma yat tat tāmasamucyate ||25||

(25) The action which is performed with delusion, regardless of the consequences, loss, injury and the individual's own ability—that is declared to be *tamasic.*

muktasaṅgo'nahaṁvādī dhṛtyutsāhasamanvitaḥ

siddhyasiddhyor nirvikāraḥ kartā sāttvika ucyate ||26||

(26) Free from attachment and the feeling of

I, who is endowed with determination and enthusiasm, who remains unaffected by success and failure—that doer is said to be *sattvic* (pure).

rāgī karmaphalaprepsurlubdho hinsātmako'śuciḥ

harṣaśokānvitaḥ kartā rājasaḥ parikīrtitaḥ ||27||

(27) The one who is swayed by passion, who eagerly seeks the fruits of his actions, who is greedy, violent, impure and who is easily moved by joy and sorrow—that doer is said to be *rajasic* (passionate).

ayuktaḥ prākṛtaḥ stabdhaḥ śaṭho naiśkṛtiko'lasaḥ

viṣādī dīrghasūtrī ca kartā tāmasa ucyate ||28||

(28) Who is unsteady, vulgar, stubborn, deceitful, malicious, lazy, despondent and procrastinating—that doer is declared to be *tamasic* (ignorant).

buddher bhedaṁ dhṛteś caiva guṇatas trividhaṁ śṛṇu

procyamānamaśeṣeṇa pṛthaktvena dhanañjaya ||29||

(29) Now hear, O'Arjuna the threefold division of intellect and also of steadiness, according to the gunas; as I declare them fully and separately.

pravṛttiṁ ca nivṛttiṁ ca kāryākārye bhayābhaye

bandhaṁ mokṣaṁ ca yā vetti buddhiḥ sā pārtha sāttvikī ||30||

(30) The intellect which determines clearly the path of activity and renunciation; what ought to be done and what should not be done; what is to be feared and what is not to be feared; what is bondage and what is freedom; O'Partha (Arjuna)—that intellect is *sattvic* (Pure).

yayā dharmamadharmaṁ ca kāryaṁ cākāryameva ca
ayathāvat prajānāti buddhiḥ sā pārtha rājasī ||31||

(31) That which gives an erroneous understanding of Dharma and Adharma, and also of what should be done and what should not be done—that intellect O'Partha is *rajasic.*

adharmaṁ dharmamiti yā manyate tamasāvṛtā
sarvārthān viparītāṅś ca buddhiḥ sā pārtha tāmasī ||32||

(32) That which perceives even Adharma to be Dharma; which is enveloped in darkness and reverses every value—that intellect O'Partha is indeed *tamasic.*

dhṛtyā yayā dhārayate manaḥ prāṇendriyakriyāḥ
yogenāvyabhicāriṇyā dhṛtiḥ sā pārtha sāttvikī ||33||

(33) The unwavering steadiness by which, through Yoga, one controls the activities of the mind, the life breath and the senses—that firmness

O'Partha is *sattvic.*

yayā tu dharmakāmarthān dhṛtyā dhārayate'rjuna

prasaṅgena phalākāṅkṣī dhṛtiḥ sā pārtha rājasī ||34||

(34) The steadiness by which one holds fast to Dharma (duty), pleasure and wealth; desiring the fruit in consequence thereof—that firmness is *rajasic,* O'Arjuna.

yayā svapnaṁ bhayaṁ śokaṁ viṣādaṁ madameva ca

na vimuñcati durmedhā dhṛtiḥ sa pārtha tāmasī ||35||

(35) That by which a fool does not abandon sleep, fear, grief, depression and conceit as well—that firmness O'Arjuna is *tamasic.*

sukhaṁ tvidānīṁ trividhaṁ śṛṇu me bharatarṣabha

abhyāsād ramate yatra duhkhāntaṁ ca nigacchati ||36||

(36) Now hear from Me, O'Arjuna, the threefold division of happiness—that in which one comes to rejoice by long practice and in which he reaches to the end of his pain.

yat tad agre viṣamiva pariṇāme'mṛtopamam

tat sukhaṁ sāttvikaṁ proktamātmabuddhiprasādajam ||37||

(37) That which is like poison in the beginning but becomes like an elixir in the end—which is born of a clear understanding of the Self, that

happiness is declared to be *sattvic.*

viṣayendriyasaṁyogād yat tadagre'mṛtopamam

pariṇāme viṣamiva tat sukhaṁ rājasaṁ smṛtam ||38||

(38) That which arises from contacts of the senses with their objects; which is at first like nectar and in the end like poison—that happiness is said to be *rajasic.*

yad agre cānubandhe ca sukhaṁ mohanamātmanaḥ

nidrālasyapramādotthaṁ tat tamasamudāhṛtam ||39||

(39) That happiness which at the beginning as well as in the end, deludes the embodied-self, through sleep, sloth and negligence—that is declared to be *tamasic.*

na tadasti pṛthivyāṁ vā divi deveṣu vā punaḥ

sattvaṁ prakṛtijair muktaṁ yadebhiḥ syāt tribhirguṇaiḥ ||40||

(40) There is no creature either on earth or in heaven among the celestials, which is free from these three qualities, born of Prakriti (Nature).

brāhmaṇakṣatriyaviśāṁ śūdrāṇāṁ ca parantapa

karmāṇi pravibhaktāni svabhāvaprabhavairguṇaiḥ ||41||

(41) Of Brahmins, Of Kshatriyas and Vaisyas as well as of Sudras, O'Arjuna, the activities are divided in accordance with their own inborn qualities of nature.

śamo damas tapaḥ śaucaṁ kṣāntirārjavameva ca

jñānaṁ vijñānamāstikyaṁ brahmakarma svabhāvajam ||42||

(42) Serenity, self-restraint, austerity, purity, forbearance, and straightforwardness; knowledge, wisdom and faith in religion—all these are the duties of a Brahmin; born of his inherent nature.

śauryaṁ tejo dhṛtirdākṣyaṁ yuddhe cāpyapalāyanam

dānamīśvarabhāvaś ca kṣātraṁ karma svabhāvajam ||43||

(43) Heroism, vigour, steadiness, fortitude, dexterity (skilfulness), and also not fleeing from battle; generosity and lordliness—are the duties of a Kshatriya, born of his inherent nature.

kṛṣigaurakṣyavāṇijyaṁ vaiśyakarma svabhāvajam

paricaryātmakaṁ karma śūdrasyāpi svabhāvajam ||44||

(44) Agriculture, cattle rearing and trade are the duties of a Vaisya, born of his nature; while the work consisting of service is the duty of a Sudra, born of his nature.

sve-sve karmaṇyabhirataḥ saṁsiddhiṁ labhate naraḥ

svakarmaniratạḥ siddhiṁ yathā vindati tacchṛṇu ||45||

(45) Sincerely devoted to his own duty, man attains the highest perfection. How he attains the perfection, being devoted to the performance of his own inborn duty; listen to that now.

yataḥ pravṛttir bhūtānāṁ yena sarvamidaṁ tatam
svakarmaṇā tamabhyarcya siddhiṁ vindati mānavaḥ ||46||

(46) He from whom all beings have evolved and by whom all this is pervaded—worshipping Him, through the performance of ones own duty, a man attains perfection.

śreyān svadharmo viguṇaḥ paradharmāt svanuṣṭhitāt
svabhāvaniyataṁ karma kurvannāpnoti kilbiṣam ||47||

(47) Better is one's own duty, though destitute of merits, than the duty of another well performed—He, who does the duty ordained by his own inherent nature, he incurs no sin.

sahajaṁ karma kaunteya sadoṣamapi na tyajet
sarvārambhā hi doṣeṇa dhūmenāgnirivāvṛtāḥ ||48||

(48) Therefore, O'son of Kunti (Arjuna) one should not abandon one's innate duty, even though it is imperfect; for, all enterprises are enveloped by imperfections, as is the fire by smoke.

asaktabuddhiḥ sarvatra jitātmā vigataspṛhaḥ
naiṣkarmyasiddhiṁ paramāṁ sannyāsenādhigacchati ||49||

(49) He, whose intellect is unattached in all respects, who is self-controlled and free from all desires—he by renunciation, attains the Supreme

state of freedom from action.

siddhiṁ prāpto yathā brahma tathāpnoti nibodha me
samāsenaiva kaunteya niṣṭhā jñānasya yā parā ||50||

(50) Know from Me, in brief, O'Arjuna, how having attained perfection, he attains to the Brahman—The Supreme consummation of knowledge.

buddhyā viśuddhayā yukto dhṛtyātmānaṁ niyamya ca
śabdādīn viṣayāns tyaktvā rāgadveṣau vyudasya ca ||51||

(51) Endowed with the purity of intellect, controlling the mind by steadfastness, relinquishing the external sounds and the other objects of senses; laying aside both attraction and aversion.

viviktasevī laghvāśī yatavākkāyamānasaḥ
dhyānayogaparo nityaṁ vairāgyaṁ samupāśritaḥ ||52||

(52) Resorting to solitude, eating but very little, controlling speech, body and mind; always engaged in Yoga of meditation and taking refuge in dispassion.

ahaṅkāraṁ balaṁ darpaṁ kāmaṁ krodhaṁ parigraham
vimucya nirmamaḥ śānto brahmabhūyāya kalpate ||53||

(53) Having abandoned egoism, violence, arrogance, lust and anger; who is free from the notion of 'mineness' and is totally at peace within—

he becomes worthy of being one with Brahman.

brahmabhūtaḥ prasannātmā na śocati na kāṅkṣati
samaḥ sarveṣu bhūteṣu madbhaktiṁ labhate parām ||54||

(54) Settled in the identity with the Brahman, cheerful in mind; he neither grieves nor desires. Regarding all beings alike, he attains Supreme devotion to Me.

bhaktyā māmabhijānāti yāvān yaś cāsmi tattvataḥ
tato māṁ tattvato jñātvā viśate tadanantaram ||55||

(55) Through devotion, he comes to know about Me, what and who I am in essence; then having known Me in truth, he forthwith enters into Me.

sarvakarmāṇyapi sadā kurvāṇo madvyapāśrayaḥ
matprasādād avāpnoti śāśvataṁ padamavyayam ||56||

(56) While performing all actions, he who always seeks refuge in Me—by My grace, he attains the eternal, immutable state.

cetasā sarvakarmāṇi mayi sannyasya matparaḥ
buddhiyogamupāśritya maccittaḥ satataṁ bhava ||57||

(57) Consciously surrendering all actions to Me, regarding Me as the Supreme goal; resorting to the Yoga of integral wisdom (Buddhi-yoga)—focus your mind constantly on Me.

maccittaḥ sarvadurgāṇi matprasādāt tariṣyasi

atha cet tvamahaṅkārān na śroṣyasi vinaṅkṣyasi ||58||

(58) Focusing thus your mind on Me—by My grace, you will overcome all the difficulties; but, if because of egoism, you will not listen to Me, thou shalt perish.

yadahaṅkāramāsritya na yotsya iti manyase

mithyaiṣa vyavasāyaste prakṛtis tvāṁ niyokṣyati ||59||

(59) If, in your self-conceit, you think "I will not fight," your resolve is in vain. Nature will compel you.

svabhāvajena kaunteya nibaddhaḥ svena karmaṇā

kartuṁ necchasi yan mohāt kariṣyasyavaśo'pi tat ||60||

(60) O'Arjuna, bound by your sense of duty (karma) born of your own inner disposition; that which from delusion, you do not desire to do, even that, you will do helplessly.

īśvaraḥ sarvabhūtānāṁ hṛddeśe'rjuna tiṣthati

bhrāmayan sarvabhūtāni yantrārūḍhāni māyayā ||61||

(61) The Lord dwells in the hearts of all beings, O'Arjuna, causing them to revolve (bound by their karmas) by His illusive power; as if they were mounted on a machine.

tameva śaraṇaṁ gaccha sarvabhāvena bhārata
tatprasādāt parāṁ śāntiṁ sthānaṁ prāpsyasi śāśvatam ||62||

(62) Take refuge in Him alone, with all your being, O'Arjuna. By His grace, you will attain the Supreme peace and the eternal abode.

iti te jñānamākhyātaṁ guhyād guhyataraṁ mayā
vimṛśyaitadaśeṣeṇa yathecchasi tathā kuru ||63||

(63) Thus, this knowledge, which is the Supreme mystery of all mysteries, has been declared to you by Me. Reflect on it fully, and then act as thou wishest.

sarvaguhyatamaṁ bhūyaḥ śṛṇu me paramaṁ vacaḥ
iṣto'si me dṛḍhamiti tato vakṣyāmi te hitam ||64||

(64) Listen, once again to My Supreme word, the profound secret of all. Since you are very dear to Me, therefore, I shall tell you, that which is good for you.

manmanā bhava madbhakto madyājī māṁ namaskuru
māmevaiṣyasi satyaṁ te pratijāne priyo'si me ||65||

(65) Focus your mind on Me, be devoted to Me, worship Me, and prostrate thyself before Me—you will come to Me alone. I promise you certainly, because you are very dear to Me.

sarvadharmān parityajya māmekaṁ śaraṇaṁ vraja

ahaṁ tvā sarvapāpebhyo mokṣayiṣyāmi mā śucaḥ ||66||

(66) Resigning all the Dharmas, seek refuge in Me alone. I shall liberate you from all sins. Grieve not.

idaṁ te nātapaskāya nābhaktāya kadācana

na cāśuśrūṣave vācyaṁ na ca māṁ yo'bhyasūyati ||67||

(67) This should not be told by you to the one, who is devoid of austerities and also who lacks devotion; or to the one who is unwilling to hear and also who finds fault with Me.

ya idaṁ paramaṁ guhyaṁ madbhakteṣvabhidhāsyati

bhaktiṁ mayi parāṁ kṛtvā māmevaiṣyatyasaṁśayaḥ ||68||

(68) He, who with Supreme devotion to Me, will teach this Supreme secret to My devotees, shall come to Me, there is no doubt about it.

na ca tasmānmanuṣyeṣu kaścin me priyakṛttamaḥ

bhavitā na ca me tasmād anyaḥ priyataro bhuvi ||69||

(69) There is none among men, who does dearer service to Me than he; nor shall there be another on earth dearer to Me than he.

adhyeṣyate ca ya imaṁ dharmyaṁ saṁvādamāvayoḥ

jñānayajñena tenāhamiṣṭaḥ syāmiti me matiḥ ||70||

(70) He, who will study this sacred dialogue of ours, by him I shall be worshipped through the *yajña* (sacrifice) of knowledge. Such is my conviction.

śraddhāvānanasūyaś ca śṛṇuyādapi yo naraḥ
sopi muktaḥ śubhāṅllokān prāpnuyāt puṇyakarmaṇām ||71||

(71) The man who listens to this with full faith and without scoffing—he too shall be liberated, and shall attain the auspicious worlds of the righteous.

kaccidetacchrutaṁ pārtha tvayaikāgreṇa cetasā
kaccidajñānasaṁmohaḥ pranaṣṭas te dhanañjaya ||72||

(72) Have you heard this gospel attentively, O'Arjuna? Has your delusion, born of ignorance been dispelled?

Arjuna Uvāca :

naṣṭo mohaḥ smṛtir labdhā tvatprasādān mayā'cyuta
sthito'smi gatasandehaḥ kariṣye vacanaṁ tava ||73||

Arjuna said :

(73) O'Kṛṣṇa, my delusion is destroyed and I have regained my memory (knowledge of the self) through your grace. Now I am totally integrated and free from all doubts. I shall act according to

Thy word.

Sañjaya Uvāca :

ityahaṁ vāsudevasya pārthasya ca mahātmanaḥ

saṁvādamimamaśrauṣamadbhutaṁ romaharṣaṇam ||74||

Sañjaya said :

(74) Thus, I have heard this most wondrous dialogue between Srī Kṛṣṇa and the highly enlightened Arjuna, which makes my hair stand on end (genuinely thrilled and blessed).

vyāsaprasādācchrutavānetad guhyamahaṁ param

yogaṁ yogeśvarāt kṛṣṇāt sākṣāt kathayataḥ svayam ||75||

(75) Through the grace of the sage Vyasa, I have heard this Supreme mystery of Yoga as declared in person by Srī Kṛṣṇa himself—the Lord of Yoga.

rājan saṅsmṛtya-saṅsmṛtya saṁvādamimamadbhutam

keśavārjunayoḥ puṇyaṁ hṛṣyāmi ca muhur-muhuḥ ||76||

(76) O'King, as I recall again and again the most wondrous and the sacred dialogue between Srī Kṛṣṇa and Arjuna I rejoice over and over again.

tacca saṅsmṛtya-saṅsmṛtya rūpamatyadbhutaṁ hareḥ

vismayo me māhān rājan hṛṣyāmi ca punaḥ-punaḥ ||77||

(77) And remembering over and over again,

that most magnificent cosmic form of Hari (Srī Kṛṣṇa); greater is indeed my amazement. O'King, I feel thrilled with joy again and again.

yatra yogeśvaraḥ kṛṣṇo yatra pārtho dhanurdharaḥ

tatra śrīr vijayo bhūtirdhruvā nītir matir mama ||78||

(78) Wherever there is Srī Kṛṣṇa, the Lord of Yoga, and wherever there is Arjuna, the wielder of the bow; there are always the glory, victory, prosperity and righteousness; such is my firm conviction.

'AUM TAT SAT'—Thus in the Upanishad of the glorious Bhagawad Geeta, the science of the Brahman (Absolute) the scripture of yoga, the dialogue between Srī Kṛṣṇa and Arjuna—thus ends the eighteenth chapter entitled "Moksasannyasa-yoga".

ŚRĪ KṚṢṆA ARPANAMASTU